The project manager who smiled

The project manager who smiled

The value of fun in project management

PETER TAYLOR

Copyright © Peter Taylor, 2013

The right of Peter Taylor to be identified as the authors of this book has
been asserted in accordance with the Copyright, Designs and Patents
Act 1988.

First published in 2013 by
The Lazy Project Manager Ltd
3 Foxwood Drive
Binley Woods
Coventry
CV3 2SP

A CIP catalogue record for this book is available from the British Library
ISBN 978–0–9576689–0–4

To Jenny; remember, some of life is serious but even these parts can be helped by a little bit of fun

Contents

Acknowledgements 9

Foreword.. 10

About the author 15

About the book 17

1. Why fun is a good thing............................... 19

2. PM celebrity gossip – carpe diem: Mark Perry 24

3. Fun inspiration 30

4. PM celebrity gossip – two languages and joke
   power: Stephen Carver 40

5. Fun jokes 45

6. PM celebrity gossip – 24 style: Kenny Phipps........... 57

7. Fun motivation.. 61

8. PM celebrity gossip – the bad parrot:
   Alfonso Bucero 76

9. Fun status.. 78

10. PM celebrity gossip – the asterisk on projects:
    Jeff Furman.. 80

11. Fun ideas 83

12. PM celebrity gossip – it's the end of the world:
    Jon Quigley.. 97

13. A fun theme tune.................................... 101

14. PM celebrity gossip – no win situations:
    Naomi Caietti....................................... 105

15. A fun team – Shell UK 110

16. PM celebrity gossip – team building with
consequences: Gary 'Gazza' Nelson...................121

17. A fun team – IHG....................................125

18. PM celebrity gossip – avoiding check-box fun:
Robert Kelly...135

19. A fun final word...................................137

The Plan...139

Appendix 1: The Giant Killer-Carrot of Death 141

Appendix 2: Peter Taylor...............................145

Appendix 3: The Lazy Project Manager...................147

Acknowledgements

Personal

This one has to go out to all of the project teams and customers I have worked with, to all of the project managers who sent me their experiences and jokes, as well as to the project management 'celebrities' for their 'PM Celebrity Gossip' contributions.

Walt Disney said 'It's kind of fun to do the impossible' but, unfortunately, many project managers seem to think, or have been trained to think, that 'It's kind of impossible to do the fun' when in reality I say 'It's kind of not possible to not do the fun when you're trying to do the impossible, or something close to the impossible'.

In my previous 'Lazy' books – *The Lazy Project Manager, The Lazy Winner* and *The Lazy Project Manager and The Project from Hell* I have included as much 'fun' as I can think of (and get away with), even in *Leading Successful PMOs* I gave it my best shot, but with this book the shackles are off and it is 100% humour all of the way.

I hope that you enjoy it and share it all with your project teams.

Peter *The Lazy Project Manager* Taylor

Foreword

Andrew Filev

In our recent survey on working habits, one of the questions that we asked 2,000 team members, managers, executives and business owners was, "What stimulates your efficiency at work?" Good mood was cited as the second strongest motivator of productivity, ranking higher than such serious factors as a possible reward or fear of superiors. Over 57% of respondents said that good mood is a very powerful motivator. Only a sense of responsibility received more votes.

This data seems to show that if we want to work on our projects in an efficient and stress-free way, a sense of fun, laughter and humor might be a tool no less powerful than detailed planning and helpful software, among many other things. Winston Churchill said, 'A joke is a very serious thing' so let's plug in a bit of science before you dive into the world of project management humour.

If we look at neuroscience research as a whole, we will find a lot of reasons why humor isn't just fun, but also healthy and useful. First, endorphins are released, which trigger positive emotions and make difficult things seem easier. I once asked one of PMI Global Congress organizers, Paula Jayne White, about the lessons learned from orchestrating such a large event. She emphasized the immense value of humor, stating, 'It's the only way to manage all of the moving parts, so that the event comes together flawlessly'.

Now, going back to neuroscience, there are also other chemical processes in the brain which make a direct impact on stress and tension reduction. Pumping some extra oxygen to the brain, laughter literally gives the brain more 'fuel' for thinking, working and learning.

At work, a good laugh not only reduces tension and relieves stress, but also helps to increase team bonding and boost morale. Many businesses, both big and small, demonstrate original ways to incorporate fun into work. For example, representatives of Volvo shared how they held online parties across distances. Say, a team from one country ordered food into the office in another location for an impromptu celebration; everyone loved it!

At Wrike, we are ahead of the curve in a very competitive market. This takes a lot of hard work, and one of our productivity 'secrets' is that humour is a large part of our culture. It keeps stress low, promotes team spirit, and boosts creativity. We create internal graphical memes that we display in our break room, fun T-shirts, and brainstorm April Fool's Day press releases. One imaginative new feature that has been discussed is a Wrike toaster that imprints your daily to-do list into your bread. Another idea is a Wrike gamification package with a bag of carrots, a stick and a collection of Boy Scout badges.

During our regular team video-conferences that bring together multiple offices, we discuss the latest achievements and future plans, with stats, graphs, mock-ups, and other more technical things. However, we also share some of our leisure photos and fun stories. It's a great way to get to know each other better so that the team is connected not just professionally, but also socially. Work is big part of our lives, and we love it.

There are many different ways in which humour can help you and your team at work. So, enjoy the abundance of fun stories in this book, smile and get inspired for creative solutions to the challenges you face on your project management journey.

Have fun and stay productive!

Andrew Filev is the founder and CEO of Wrike, a leading provider of project management software that makes daily work easy and stress-free for thousands of companies. Andrew started his first software development business at the age of 18. Today, he is a seasoned software entrepreneur, project and product manager, and advisor to several fast-growing ventures. You can learn more about Andrew's views on project management, business and technology in his Project Management 2.0 blog (www.wrike.com/projectmanagement) and guest articles he contributes to tech and business media (VentureBeat, PandoDaily, etc.)

Wrike provides the best-in-class solution for completing multiple projects with co-located or distributed teams of any size. The perfect mix of project management and collaboration features makes Wrike a win-win choice for both managers and their teams, helping them to achieve a new level of productivity at work smoothly and easily. Wrike is trusted by many of the world's leading brands, which rely on Wrike in managing their day-to-day work. As more and more businesses choose Wrike, the company shows stable, triple-digit growth year-to-year. Try Wrike's solution for stress-free project management at **www.wrike.com**

Alexander Kjerulf

What do you want out of your work life? Think about that for a second.

If your answer is 'a steady pay check and peace and quiet until retirement' then don't bother to read this book. You can just go right ahead and join the army of disillusioned, cynical zombies slogging through their work life in a permanent state of ennui, though why anyone would want to, I'll never understand.

But hopefully your answer goes a little something like this:

'I want to kick butt at work, deliver great and successful projects and make a difference. I want to wake up in the morning excited to go to work and have a great time while I'm there. I want to be an inspiration to my co-workers and everyone around me – I want them to be happy that I'm there. I want to come home from work fulfilled and with energy to enjoy my family, friends and my life.'

If this is you then this is the book for you. And what's more, I salute you for having the stones to go against the grain and deciding to actually enjoy your work life and just have some 'fun'.

Think about it: You will spend a third of your life at work. You'll spend more of your waking hours at work than on anything else, including friends and family. Make those hours count. Make them enjoyable and fun. And make sure that the results that come out of those hours are worthy of your time.

And this is not soft, idealistic, naive, hippie thinking. This is about enjoying work, certainly, but it's also about success. Because people who are happy at work do better work. When you're happy, you are more productive, more creative, more open, more likeable and a better leader. You're also less stressed and get sick less often.

This also means that there's a business pay-off to happiness. In short, happy people make for successful projects and successful projects, along with all of those happy people, make happy companies which guess what? Make more money.

So read this book and learn how you can enjoy work more and be more successful. And why anyone wouldn't want that, I'll never understand!

Alexander Kjerulf is the founder of Woohoo inc and one of the world's leading experts on happiness at work. He is a speaker, consultant and author, presenting and conducting workshops on happiness at work at businesses and conferences all over the world. Alex is the author of 3 books including the international bestseller Happy Hour is 9 to 5 (How to Love Your Job, Love Your Life and Kick Butt at Work). You can find out more about Alex and his work at **www.positivesharing.com**

About the author

Serious

Peter Taylor is a dynamic and commercially astute professional who has achieved notable success in Project Management.

His background is in project management and marketing across three major business areas over the last 28 years, with the last 8 years leading PMOs.

He is also an accomplished communicator and a professional speaker, workshop trainer and consultant, and a coach focusing on PMO/PM guidance – Experience: Creativity: Motivation. Book him for your next event or training activity.

Peter is the author of *The Lazy Project Manager*, The Lazy Winner' and *The Lazy Project Manager and the Project from Hell* (Infinite Ideas), as well as 'Leading Successful PMOs' (Gower) and 'Project Branding' (RMC Publications) and 'Strategies for Project Sponsorship' (Management Concepts).

More information can be found at www.thelazyprojectmanager.com and www.leadingsuccessfulpmos.com and www.thelazywinner.com and www.strategies4sponsors.com – and through his free podcasts in iTunes.

If you would like to learn even more then Peter can be contacted for articles, training, workshops, presentations and keynotes at peter.b.taylor@btinternet.com

Fun

Peter Taylor is a recovering second generation Virgo with a penchant for occasionally dressing up as a root vegetable (see The Giant Killer Carrot of Death later on) and generally getting bored when there hasn't been a laugh or a smile within the last 60 minutes.

His hobbies include trying to appear in the background of as many tourist photos as possible without getting spotted (apologies if you have a deranged Brit leaping up in the background of one of your treasured holiday snaps) and negotiating the release of his home from the squatters that his wife refers to as 'the children'.

Peter is also the author of *The Dance of the Meerkats* – his attempt at a children's book – and *The Lazy Blogger* (self-published) – his attempt at going it alone - as well as this book *The project manager who smiled* – his attempt at convincing everyone else that you just have to laugh.

About the book

I do really believe in all of this fun stuff you know. Time flies when you are having fun and project work gets delivered, and delivered well, when the project team is having a jolly good time.

This book is packed full with ideas and jokes, inspirational thoughts and quotes, suggestions and maxims, anecdotes and all manner of good material that I just know you will steal and use in your own projects – and that is exactly what I want you to do.

Go ahead and don't be shy out there – fill yer boots!

In between all of my personal thoughts and the great submissions I received from project managers all over the world there are some superb contributions under the heading of 'PM Celebrity Gossip' from some project management experts that I have had the pleasure of meeting, and in some cases, working with, in the past. I know you will love these.

And there are two fabulous case studies of organisations 'walking' with joy on the fun side of the project world, and not only that, seeing some real return on the investment as a result.

'Fun is good'

Dr. Seuss

1
Why Fun is a good thing

How many project managers does it take to change a light bulb?

A better question to ask is perhaps 'how many project managers does it take to have a good project?'

I think just the one, if they have a real sense of humour and an appreciation for the value of 'fun' in a project team.

Richard Branson, Virgin Group said 'Have fun, success will follow. If you aren't having fun, you are doing it wrong. If you feel like getting up in the morning to work on your business is a chore, then it's time to try something else. If you are having a good time, there is a far greater chance a positive, innovative atmosphere will be nurtured ... A smile and a joke can go a long way, so be quick to see the lighter side of life'.

And fun is definitely out there in project management world. When I asked for contributions to this book from all of my social contacts[1] 'Author is seeking stories and experiences from the lighter side of project management' I received this reply via Twitter from @PMOPlanet 'I'm afraid with my waistline, I'm on the heavier side of project management, as opposed to the lighter side'.

In my first book *The Lazy Project Manager* I dedicated a chapter to 'Having Fun' (perhaps one of the first project management

---

1 The author can be found lurking on Twitter as @thelazypm, on LinkedIn as 'Peter Taylor' and on the web as *The Lazy Project Manager* or *The Lazy Winner*. He is not on Facebook because it is clearly evil and his wife might notice what he gets up to.

books to do so?) and stated 'You have to laugh; well I think you have to laugh. Without a little bit of fun in every project then the project world can be a dark and depressing place. Setting a professional but fun structure for your project can really be beneficial for when the problems start to rise up to challenge your plan of perfectness. And problems will inevitably arise'.

And I know as I have travelled the world and presented at many conferences and congresses that the humour that I put into my keynote presentations makes them popular, enjoyable and, as a result, it gets the message to the audience. There is nothing worse than 60 minutes of fact based detail being presented in a monotone voice without the slightest glimmer of a smile.

There is the commonly shared piece of wisdom that declares that 'it takes more muscles to frown than to smile'? Well it is rubbish. You will hear a whole range of numbers of muscles used but the truth is that medically there is no such balance for or against the 'smile' but what is a universal truth was proven in a Swedish study back in 2002 that confirmed what we already knew[2] and that is people respond in kind to the facial expressions that they encounter. If it was a frown then a frown was returned, if it was a smile then it was a smile that was returned automatically. Interestingly when the subjects of the test were asked to respond to a smile with a frown, or a frown with a smile they really struggled.

So, it isn't any easier to be a happy face rather than a grumpy face but a happy face generally engendered a whole lot of other happy faces.

And what do happy faces make? Well a lot of things it seems.

Happy, positive people tend to live longer apparently:

A number of studies have shown that happy people tend to live longer. One study looked at a group of nuns who wrote a

---

2   Actually an awful lot of these studies seem to 'prove' what we already know.

short biographical sketch before taking their vows. At the age of 85, 90% of the nuns with 'cheerful' biographies were still alive compared to 54% of the least 'cheerful'.

So be positive and you might make it to the end of that never-ending project.

Happy, positive people have the 'bounce back' factor:

It seems that happiness and an attitude of optimism tend to go hand in hand. Optimistic people see bad things as only temporary and good things as mostly permanent. Their positive expectation helps them see and act on opportunities faster and to overcome set-backs easier.

So be positive and you can deal with all of that [insert expletive of your choice here] that heads your way on the projects from hell[3].

Happy, positive people are better teamies:

There is also a strong link between feeling good and doing good. Studies have shown that happy people are more willing to help others, so happy people make the world a better place.

So be positive and your project team members will be all the better for it.

Happy, positive people feel pretty good about it all:

Let's face it, we all get a good feeling when we feel positive and upbeat, it is infectious isn't it? The better that we feel the more we achieve and get on with others and, as a direct result, we feel even more positive.

Linked to that if we choose work that we like to do and that is meaningful to us, and that is challenging as well, it can generate those peak moments of enjoyment.

So be positive and enjoy your chosen profession of project management.

And, as I say in *The Lazy Project Manager*, the right sort of

---

3   And talking of Project from Hell – have you checked out **www. theprojectfromhell.com** yet?

'fun' project environment can be good for you as well, 'Done right you will have set the acceptable parameters for fun in your project, both in content and in extent, and you will have engendered that spirit amongst your project team to the point where, one day, when you are the one on a low, they will come up and make you smile.'

Be Happy – Have Fun!

'Humour is by far the most significant activity of the human brain'

Edward de Bono

2
PM Celebrity Gossip[4] – Carpe diem: Mark Perry

Years ago, I learned at first hand the importance and value in the context of a large, mega project of seizing the day or if I borrow the Latin phrase from Horace, 'carpe diem'[5]. At the time, I was the Asia Pacific managing director for a telecommunications industry software firm and we had a very large, 18 month, complex project with a client in Japan. In my formal role as managing director, I was the project executive to the client and interfaced directly with the CEO and executive team of the client.

On a Monday morning in Tokyo we were set to have a project kick-off meeting with the CEO and top leadership team. All of the important people from the client side were there and in addition to my team, we were also flying our business partner from India responsible for the Double Byte Character Set (DBCS) enablement portion of the project which was the main part of the agenda. All of the client leadership team members had arrived for the meeting and my local team was there too, but we were missing our DBCS expert from India. We had tea

---

4   My thanks to all of the PM 'celebs' who provided some great personal stories – I enjoyed them all as I am sure you, the reader, will do as well. My thanks also to the individuals who provided jokes, and stories, and experiences that make up a lot of this book.

5   Carpe diem is a phrase from a Latin poem by Horace that is now popularly translated as 'seize the day'.

and engaged in conversations for over an hour, but still no DBCS expert from India. After about an hour, we called the meeting off so that we could find our missing DBCS expert and of course, reschedule the meeting as soon as possible.

We discovered that our DBCS expert did board his flight from India to Tokyo with a connection in Singapore, but he did not arrive in Tokyo. It was as if he just disappeared into thin air. As managing director and project executive for this project, I took the lead in trying to find out what happened. Monday came and went with no helpful information. Tuesday came and went and we were still clueless and dumbfounded as to the disappearance of our DBCS expert. Finally by end of day Wednesday, we had found out what had happened.

As it so happens, the Singapore Air flight from India to Singapore was overbooked in economy class, so our DBCS expert from India was upgraded to first class where, upon taking his seat, he was served free-flow Champagne. This being the first time that this software engineer had flown Singapore Air, not to mention flown it in first class, he was a bit overtaken by the experience. After about his 8th glass of champagne and somewhere in between India and Singapore at 35,000 feet in the air, the DBCS expert took it upon himself to fondle the breasts of the Singapore Air stewardess. Back then they weren't called flight attendants.

Well, you can only imagine what happened next. The DBCS expert from India was arrested upon arrival in Singapore and sent to jail where he remained for three days before he was allowed to make a phone call. In his defence, Singapore Air did serve him too much Champagne and surely they should take some responsibility for that. And, the first class stewardesses were all tall and very beautiful with flowing long, silky hair, and ever so 'je ne sais quoi' - surely they too should bear some of the blame. In fact, as someone who has a Singaporean wife, I would suggest that they bear ALL of the blame, but I digress.

So, back in Tokyo, it is now Thursday morning and I finally have news of what happened to report back to the CEO of our client. He welcomes me into his enormous office and asks if I have an update on what happened to our DBCS expert. In fact, his very words were, 'Perry-san, do you have update?'

I had been thinking about ways to communicate the essence of what I had learned, but without going into all of the details, but the story just didn't make sense unless it was disclosed in full. I could not think of any other thing to do or say than to tell him exactly the facts that I had learned. I took a deep breath and related all that I had found out. After I finished with the story, the CEO asked me to remain in his office and, expressionless, he leaves the office and after a few minutes which seemed like an eternity returns with his entire executive team. Once they all have been seated, the CEO turns his attention my way and gently commands, 'Perry-san, please tell leadership team what you told me, word for word.'

A bit worried that I might leave something out, I try to repeat the story word for word – DBCS expert upgraded to first class, has too much to drink, fondles breast of Singapore Air stewardess, arrested upon landing in Singapore, thrown in jail for 3 days without being able to make a phone call, negotiated release of DBCS expert from prison in exchange for permanent deportation, have new DBCS expert flying up to Tokyo as we speak, etc.

After I finish the story, there is dead silence and a dozen emotionless stares all in my direction. And then, as if on cue, the entire executive team roared in laughter. One of the executives laughed and said, 'Perry-san, you should fly JAL (Japan Airlines). On JAL, in first class, it is okay to fondle breasts[6].' One after another executive chimed in with a similar

6   This is, of course, absolutely untrue and no sexism is intended by this story;

response and confirmation of the permitted behavior. After the laughter subsided, the CEO suggested that this would be a good time to break for lunch. After all, it was 10:45am..!

We proceeded to a traditional Japanese, sit on the floor style, restaurant where we ate raw seafood and drank Sake through the afternoon. The time passed by quickly as the executive team told one project story after another. At 4pm sharp, the CEO sat up just a bit, signalling all others to come to attention. At the time, I had no idea what was happening as I was under the influence of more than one too many sakes.

The CEO announced to the others, 'This has been a very good day and a very good start to a long, complex project that will no doubt have many difficulties far greater than a first class flight on Singapore Air. This start should serve as a reminder that we should expect problems on this project, but we WILL deliver this project successfully. I am counting on the very best efforts of each and every one of you. I look forward to tomorrow's meeting with our new DBCS expert from India.' With that the day was ended.

Over the course of the project, there were many project difficulties and tough challenges. But the entire project team and all involved never lost their sense of dedication to the project nor did they lose their sense of humor. Had the CEO reacted differently to the initial project start and memorable mishap, the project could have easily started out on a very bad note. Instead, the CEO saw the folly of it all. And in response, he seized the day and turned an event that could have been a bad omen for the project into a team building event that both immediately bonded us as a dedicated team and reminded us to be prepared for and to overcome the many challenges that were no doubt lying in wait for us. Project Management Carpe Diem.

---

it is just that, a story of what happened on one project with one group of people.

Mark Price Perry is a PMO advocate and thought contributor in the PMO domain with over three decades of PMO and project management related experience. In 1999, Perry founded BOT International, a boutique firm that specializes in PMO content assets and PMO setup services and has worked with PMOs in over 40 countries. Perry is the author of Business Driven PMO Setup *(2009),* Business Driven Project Portfolio Management *(2011), and* Business Driven PMO Success Stories *(2012) all published by J. Ross Publishing.*

'Most of the time I don't have much fun. The rest of the time I don't have any fun at all'

Woody Allen

3
Fun inspiration

I am now going to hand over for short while (in my typical productive lazy manner) to Wayne Turk, who is a retired Air Force lieutenant colonel and government contractor. He has managed projects for DoD, other federal agencies, and non-profit organizations and was a frequent contributor to Defense AT&L from which this is an extract from two articles he put together, and I thank him for letting me use the great material in this book.

Project Managers as a group seem to take themselves way too seriously. That's understandable. They have to deal with unreasonable expectations, unrealistic schedules, unworkable budgets, too few resources and crises that seem to pop up on a daily basis. You have to question why anyone would want the job and the stress level that goes with it. I know that there have been times when I questioned myself on my career choice. One way to deal with that stress, though, is to add a little bit of humour.

Joel Goodman, in one of a number of articles from the HUMOR Project[7], points out that you need to take your job seriously ...

---

7   The HUMOR Project, Inc. is the first organization in the world to focus full-time on the positive power of humor. The mission is to make a difference by being a unique, pioneering, and cutting-edge organization that touches the lives of individuals, organizations, and nations. They seek to help people get more smileage out of their lives and jobs by applying the practical, positive power of humor and creativity. See **www.humorproject. com**

and take yourself lightly. He quotes Don Seibert, former chief executive officer and chairman of the board of the JC Penney Company as saying 'Humour helps you to keep your head clear when you're dealing in highly technical information or difficult decisions where choices aren't that clear'. That last part sounds like a typical part of Project Management to me.

Goodman also says that you can be a serious professional without being a solemn professional. To illustrate this, he quotes the very successful former manager of the New York Yankees, Casey Stengel. When asked his secret for winning, Casey replied 'The secret of managing is to keep the five guys who hate you away from the four... who are undecided'. Goodman emphasizes that humor can help us to survive – and thrive – at work. I think that he is right.

In over 30 years of management experience, I've seen that humour can be a life saver and even a career saver. Once I lightened up and added a sense of humour, it made a world of difference to my attitude and my health. During my career, I've also collected a few humorous, alright – twisted, rules concerning Project Management that have helped me keep a sometimes irreverent attitude toward my chosen field. You might want to remember that there could be an ounce or two of truth in them. For example, there are two rules about mistakes. Mistakes are going to happen on your project; so:

Never make the same mistake twice in succession ... always make at least one intervening mistake.

And that leads to the corollary:

When your goal is to keep from repeating a mistake, you are sure to make a doozie[8].

When you've made that doozie of a mistake, there is another rule:

---

8   English slang origin from the eighteenth century on, for something that was particularly appealing or excellent. It moved into North American English in the early nineteenth century.

Carry bad news to the boss the day that his promotion is announced.

Don't you wish that you could time it that well?

There are many articles written about standardization, processes, rules for success, and similar things that could make people believe there is a cookie cutter approach to Project Management that will always lead to success. There is no single approach that guarantees success. In the real world, versus the world of management theory and advice, there are some other rules concerning projects that you might want to remember.

Like these about the similarity of projects:

* Twins occur in one out of every 93 births in humans, but never with projects.
* If you try to mimic the last successful project, you are destined to be a chapter in a Lessons Learned Book.

You don't want to be held up as a bad example, so treat each project as an individual, unique entity. Yes, there are general concepts and guidelines for every project, but each project is different – different people involved, different planned outcomes, and different problems. Be careful about treating all projects the same or you might end up as the point of a Dilbert comic strip.

Even identical twins have different finger prints.

Here are a few other random rules and thoughts to go with them:

* Once a project is fouled up, anything done to improve it makes it worse. Not true, but it sure does seem that way.
* Whatever happens, behave as though you meant it to happen. Confidence and a cool façade will fool all of the people some of the time and some of the people all of the time, to paraphrase old Abe[9].

---

9   Abraham Lincoln was the 16th President of the United States, serving from March 1861 until his assassination in April 1865. He successfully led his country through its greatest constitutional, military, and moral crisis,

- The first place to look for information is in the section of the manual where you least expect to find it. Ain't it the truth? So don't write the manuals for your project that way.
- A complex system that does not work is invariably found to have evolved from a simpler system that worked just fine. Another one with more than a grain of truth I am sorry to say. Apply the KISS factor whenever possible – Keep It Simple, Stupid!
- There is never enough time to do it right the first time, but there is always enough time to do it over. We all know this one. Try not to apply it to your project.
- A carelessly planned project will take three times longer to complete than expected. A carefully planned project will only take twice as long. Okay, that one is exaggerated, but if you don't plan carefully, it is a guarantee that you won't make the timeline. Good planning is critical to a project's success.

And of course everyone knows Murphy's Law - If anything can go wrong it will - however there are other laws floating around out there in the PM world.

Here are a few that seem to be true rather too often:

- If it can't possibly go wrong, it still will – O'Malley's corollary to Murphy's Law
- Murphy and O'Malley are optimists – Zook's Law
- When it goes wrong, it will do so in the worst possible way – Sod's Law
- Work expands to fill the time available for its completion – Parkinson's Law

---

the American Civil War, preserving the Union while ending slavery, and promoting economic and financial modernization. Full quote is 'You can fool some of the people all of the time, and all of the people some of the time, but you cannot fool all of the people all of the time'.

- A two-year project will take three years, a three-year project will never finish – Turk's Law
- The more time you spend in reporting on what you are doing, the less time you have to do anything. Stability is achieved when you spend all your time doing nothing but reporting on the nothing you are doing – Cohn's Law
- Project Managers will not get the staff they need as long as they succeed through overtime, ulcers and superhuman effort. Only when deadlines are missed will senior management approve the staff who, had they been available at the outset, would have prevented the missed deadlines – Woehlke's Law

And finally, one that goes back a ways, but is still appropriate:

'And it ought to be remembered that there is nothing more difficult to take in hand, more perilous to conduct, or more uncertain in its success, than to take the lead in the introduction of a new order of things. Because the innovator has for enemies all those who have done well under the old conditions, and lukewarm defenders in those who may do well under the new' Niccolo Machiavelli

Hopefully there is something here that brought a smile to your face and lowered your stress level for a few minutes. Joel Goodman has the right idea: use humour as a tool. It can be a helpful and healthful addition to your toolkit and should be a part of your project management style.

Humour will always be subjective, though. It is easy to overstep the bounds and hurt someone's feelings or say something objectionable while trying to be funny. So think a little before you crack a joke. Be reasonably politically correct and sensitive to others. It can be difficult, but what about project management isn't?

Laughter reduces stress, eases tension and makes those unreasonable expectations, unrealistic schedules, unworkable budgets, too few resources and crises that seem to pop up on a daily basis a little easier to take.

So get to work – and smile.

OK, back to me now, thanks Wayne and what about some other contributions from project managers around the world, what has been their experience and how fun was it?

Risk Management

In my last role our prime contractor (who will remain nameless but were, shall we say, French) had a very particular approach to risk management within the programme.

As a dutiful prime contractor we produced all of our project management plans after contract award as per the contract. We then produced our risk log which we jointly reviewed in the first progress meeting, all good.

The response from our prime was that none of these risks were risks as they were all covered by contractual requirements which we were contractually bound to deliver! We then had to remove all of these risks and just manage them internally. That's certainly one approach to risk management.

Graham Herries

Reporting

I worked on a project with a steering committee where, when the project leader was reporting project status to the sponsor, he had this marvellous response: 'Don't worry; the project is progressing faster than it is getting behind schedule'.

Jean-François Bonnefous

This goes back to when Dave Shirley and I (now, nearly

respectable co-authors of the Cleland Award-winning book *Green Project Management*) were both in the same company. At the time we both led project management groups. We worked for an old-fashioned Director who wanted printed project reports of various kinds, all based on the same set of data – information by customer, by date, by priority, by product type, by project manager. We tried to explain to him that the information was right there in Excel on one sheet and all he had to do was view it in different ways, and that there wasn't any need to print it. We tried in many ways to convince him that the many reports were really just a waste of time and paper.

He persisted, though. He asked and cajoled and begged and requested and petitioned. So we shook our heads, and tended to provide him what he wanted – individual reports, tailored to his needs. Same data, just sifted in different ways according to his whim.

One fine April Fool's day, (1st April) as is the tradition in the US[10], we decided do a small prank. We chose to write up a nifty report of all of the reports we generate for him. We called it the 'Report Report'. Ostensibly, this was to illustrate how ridiculous the requests were and how much time it was taking us to do this. We meticulously illustrated for each report – in true Communications Management Plan form – the data source, in what media it would be delivered, when, how often, to whom, for what intent. Of course he was always the audience; the information source was always the same, making our point crystal clear. Except, that is, to precisely one person, the target of our prank, the recipient of our poignant underlying message.

So his reaction, rather than the 'a-ha' moment we expected followed by the "no need to generate all these reports anymore, gentlemen" was instead followed by 'This report is fantastic. I'd like to see copies of it Tuesday and Thursday of every week'

---

10 And in the UK as well I should say.

The April Fool was on us.

Moral of the story: be careful what you report on: you just may get it.'

Rich Maltzman and Dave Shirley

Communication

In a large group discussion over project diligence and rules of engagement our director made a comment that none of the team were familiar with.

He said 'There are two things you never want to see being made, law and sausages.'

Unfortunately due to poor acoustics and ambient noise in the meeting the entire team mistakenly interpreted his comment as 'There are two things you never want to see being made; long sausages' and although puzzled none of us challenged his statement.

At the break I asked the director what the second item was and shared my interpretation; he quickly explained his real comment with some surprise that nobody had commented on his curious statement to the team. After adjournment he promptly clarified his statement to a round of laughter just to ensure us all he was not crazy.

Lessons learned: You can't always believe what you hear. If you are not sure ask questions. Always doubt that your director might not be crazy.'

Cam Tennant

Many years ago I used to drive to and from Paris regularly with a colleague and so we used to share the driving. On one trip back home we were trying to be super-efficient and were doing a voice conference as we were driving back. After stopping for a short break at a service area before getting the Euro Tunnel, I pulled off on the wrong side of the road in front of a police car. The rest of the people on the call were in hysterics as they overheard the discussion re driving license, open the boot etc.

Lesson learned: Focus on what your primary task is!

Duncan Chappell

Planning

I have two stories from when I managed an application development team working as a contract Project Manager at Microsoft.

The first one occurred during my very first conference call with the entire team. It was early morning for me and early evening for them. After we did introductions of everyone over there, I introduced myself and talked about what my role was on the project. One of the things I mentioned as part of my role as the project manager was to maintain the schedule and identify any risks associated with that. So in that vein, I asked the team if anyone was planning any vacation, time-off, engagements or weddings. I further stated that I really needed to know about any planned weddings because I was aware that, many times, those affairs ran sometimes a month or longer and I needed to be sure and plan the work accordingly, or have someone come in to be a temporary replacement. When the team stated that they didn't have any of those planned at this time, I then stated that I would also like to know if anyone planned to be sick or die in the near future because I would also have to plan for that too. There was a pause and then the some chatter in the background before the team started to laugh at my comment. Then a voice spoke up and said, 'Bob, nobody has any of those plans at this time.'

The second one occurred about three months later when one of the team announced that they had just become engaged.

After all of the congratulations dies down, I asked if there was date set yet for the wedding because I had to make sure that we planned accordingly for his long absence due to what will probably be one of those month long weddings. When the response was that the wedding date had not been planned yet, I paused and then told him 'OK. When the two mothers and any other folks involved with the wedding get together, I will set up a conference call so that I can make sure that they plan the date at a good time for the project because I know who is really in control of that'.

After a short silence, the team member responded with 'I have already told my mother but you have to tell her mother because I am scared of her!' to which everyone erupted into laughter.'

Robert J. (Bob) Vandenberg

4
PM Celebrity Gossip – Two languages and Joke power: Stephen Carver

Imagine the scene; the flamboyant CEO of our US parent company was flying over the pond on the red eye special to 'address the troops' for the first time in London. London management had hired a sports hall, a working breakfast was ready and 500 of the key staff were lined up in best suits to hear the strategic future spelt out from the lips of the head man himself.

By the scheduled start time of 09.00 there was an expectant air in the hall but no sign of the CEO and no news - things were beginning to get tense. Finally at 09.30 the big man burst into the hall red faced, and obviously in a 'bit of a state'. He steamrollered onto the stage, and without any preamble launched into his first words:

'I am pissed, completely pissed. I fly a lot, and often get pissed but this morning I am about as pissed as I ever have been. I expect that most of you are pissed as well and I can assure you that this is not a good start to my announcement of our five year strategy, but here goes ...'

There was a shocked and somewhat awed silence from the audience for the next 30 minutes after which the CEO finished his speech by announcing:

'Well I hope that you are now not as pissed as you were

30 minutes ago, I'm leaving right away to have lunch with representatives of the UK Government, I'm now running late so I expect that they will all be pissed by the time I arrive'.

After the CEO had left, the UK Divisional Head discretely explained that the CEO's plane had been delayed, he had lost his phone, had been held up in immigration and perhaps most importantly 'pissed' in Texas USA meant angry, whereas in the UK is just meant 'really drunk'.

And another story.

150 miles offshore in stormy seas things were getting serious – very, very serious.

We had just got the brand new offshore platform up, running and 'on demand' for the first time, we were sending huge quantities of gas into the onshore gas network and the dollars were rolling in.

Suddenly, and without warning the platform Emergency Shutdown Panel executed a level 4 shutdown – total subsea well isolation, subsequent electrical power failure and immediate 'headless chicken' impersonations by the commissioning team. The single diesel emergency generator kicked in and some of the lights flickered back into life. Almost immediately 'the beach' (mainland operations) radioed in - 'What's happened, where's the gas? What's the problem? – get back on line!'

Whilst the team tried to find the fault, the OIM (Offshore Installation Manager - equivalent of a ship's captain) turned to me (the senior electrical officer) and 'explained' that he wanted full power back on, and now! I pointed out that without gas we had no gas turbines and without gas turbines – no power. Whilst we contemplated our tricky situation the mechanical engineer helpfully pointed out that not only did we have only 24 hours diesel capacity but also that the bearings on the diesel where inexplicably getting mighty hot and that the generator might have to be pulled offline in the next four hours. He also added that the nasty weather meant that there would be no diesel fuel, boats, parts or helicopters coming our way for 24 hours. Beyond 24 hours we would be down to battery power, and beyond that the platform would be officially declared 'dead' and would have to be evacuated – embarrassing and expensive!

My electrical team swung into action and we found some welding generator sets on deck that might just act as a stop gap alternative power supply – the only problem was that they were mismatched and missing parts – the race was on to get them online ASAP! Three hours later the 6 members of my team were stressed, exhausted and nowhere near getting the alternative power on line.

At this point one of team told one of the most corny[11] jokes I had ever heard and one by one we started giggling. Within one minute we were all caught up in a hysterical outburst that had us firstly crying with laughter and then physically rolling around the floor. Suddenly the module door opened and in strode the OIM. I can only imagine what went through his mind as he surveyed his top electrical team apparently incoherently laughing in the middle of one of the most serious situations most of us had ever known. All of us stopped dead.

To his eternal credit he simply nodded, turned round and left; quietly closing the door behind him. Sixty minutes later we had solved the problem, we then repaired the emergency generator and swiftly got the platform safely back on line. To this day I can't remember the joke but I do remember the creative power of laughter and the brilliant management call of the OIM.

As Einstein once pointed out 'creativity = intelligent people + laughter'.

---

11 Corny: Banal, commonplace, dull, feeble, hackneyed, maudlin, mawkish, old-fashioned, old hat, sentimental, stale, stereotyped, trite

Stephen Carver is rated as one of the top 3 lecturers at one of Europe's top MBA Business Schools. He has a reputation of taking complex management concepts such as Project, Programme and Crisis Management and being able to distil them down, into highly informative and fun lectures – often using 'storytelling' techniques. His attitude is 'if you haven't done it – you shouldn't be teaching it!'

Unusually, for an academic, he has actually has spent most of his working life in real business managing projects from oil rigs to bank trading systems .He still runs his own, highly successful, Project Management Company (his client list now reads like the FTSE/Dow top 100!)

Stephen believes that that a good way of predicting the success of a project is to count the smiles and laughter at meetings.

'If a man insisted always on being serious, and never allowed himself a bit of fun and relaxation, he would go mad or become unstable without knowing it'

Herodotus

5
Fun jokes

The power of humour is manifold but here is one real life tale of how one man used humour in an accomplished way:

I had the privilege early on my project management career of working with an excellent Program Director whose name escapes me, let's call him David. David's career prior to entering the commercial world was under the sea for six months at a time as the XO of a nuclear submarine. This experience brought a certain decisiveness and disregard for space that often saw David squeeze meetings of up to 20 people in his six by ten foot office.

David was far from a sergeant major type and a number of my peers took him as being an ineffective director. His management style could easily be regarded as relaxed. We wouldn't see David for days on end only for him to come wandering into the program office unannounced, stand in a strategic position, and deliver a quick and effective joke. He would then wander off leaving us in stitches.

It wasn't until a few years later that I realised what David was doing when he delivered his jokes to us. He was using humour to gauge and at times boost the morale of his program office. His jokes also served another purpose: to keep the door between David's governance function and his reports firmly open. We all knew that if a problem was big enough then we could bring them to David for a considered hearing.

The use of humour in this office created the opportunity for a productive emotional release that encouraged the building of coherent team structures in a positive way.

I have learnt a lot from David about considering and building emotional connections within my teams / decision makers that I still use today. The result of building these connections is solid teams that are purposeful and engaged to achieve the end goal. Of course, this approach is one of a number of approaches we use as effective managers to deliver the required result although we often neglect it to our detriment.

It only takes a well-timed joke or smile to turn a person's world around.

Darrin Brinsden

Perhaps some of the following jokes are ones that 'David' used, if not then here's some new material.

Some of the jokes that I enjoy

I have used these jokes a number of times in my presentations and in my first book *The Lazy Project Manager*, they always goes down well:

A Project Manager and her principal architect and her chief analyst were having a lunch time stroll along the beach, as you do, when they happened upon a small brass lamp lying on the sand. Eagerly they grabbed the lamp and rubbed it and, of course, as in every fairy tale, the giant genie appeared in a puff of magic smoke.

'I am the genie of the lamp' he proclaimed 'and I will grant you three wishes'

He paused, as if noting for the first time that there were in fact three people staring at him.

'As there are three of you then you will have to share the traditional three wishes. Each of you will be granted one wish each. Who's first?' he asked

The ever eager principal architect did not hesitate a second. 'I wish that I was on a tropical island with sun, sand, clear blue water and palm trees, oh and with a group of nubile girls delivering endless cocktails.'

'No problem' said the Genie, and with a quick flash and a puff of smoke the architect disappeared.

'Wow' said the chief analyst 'I wish I was in fast and expensive sports car driving through the mountains to my magnificent villa overlooking the Mediterranean, where I will drink champagne and eat caviar.'

'Easy' said the Genie, and with another quick flash and another puff of smoke the analyst disappeared as well.

'And what is your wish?' commanded the genie to the project manager.

'Simple' she replied 'I want those other two back at their desks by 1:30 prompt!'

This one is popular as well:

A man in a hot air balloon was lost. He reduced altitude and spotted another woman below. He descended a little bit more and shouted:

'Excuse me madam, can you help? I promised a friend I would meet him an hour ago, but I don't know where I am.'

The woman replied: 'You are in a hot air balloon hovering approximately 30 feet above alkali desert scrub habitat, 2.7 miles west of the Colorado River near one of the remnant populations and spawning grounds of the razorback sucker.'

'You must be a biologist' said the balloonist.

'I am' replied the woman. 'How did you know?'

'Well' answered the balloonist 'everything you told me is technically correct, but I have no idea what to make of your information, and the fact is I am still lost. Frankly, you've not been much help so far.'

The woman below responded 'You must be a project manager'. 'I am' replied the balloonist 'but how did you know?'

'Well, said the woman 'you don't know where you are or where you're going. You have risen to where you are due to a large quantity of hot air. You made a promise to someone that you have no idea how to keep, and you expect me to solve your problem. The fact is, you are in exactly the same position you were in before we met, but somehow it's now my fault!'

Here are a few more that you might like (they featured in *The Lazy Project Manager and the Project from Hell*)

- The nicest thing about not planning is that failure comes as a complete surprise and is not preceded by a period of worry and depression.
- A risk is something nasty you smell and an issue is something nasty you stand in.
- It takes one woman nine months to have a baby. It cannot be done in one month by impregnating nine women.
- Any project can be estimated accurately (once it's completed).
- The most valuable and least used word in a project manager's vocabulary is 'No'.
- The most valuable and least used phrase in a project manager's vocabulary is 'I don't know'.
- Nothing is impossible for the person who doesn't have to do it.
- Too few people on a project can't solve the problems - too many create more problems than they solve.
- A user will tell you anything you ask about, but nothing more.
- Right answers to wrong questions are just as wrong as wrong answers to right questions.
- What you don't know hurts you.
- There's never enough time to do it right first time but there's

always enough time to go back and do it again.
- Anything that can be changed will be changed until there is no time left to change anything.
- Change is inevitable - except from vending machines.
- The person who says it will take the longest and cost the most is the only one with a clue how to do the job.
- The bitterness of poor quality lingers long after the sweetness of meeting the date is forgotten.
- What is not on paper has not been said.
- If you don't know where you're going, any road will take you there.
- If you fail to plan you are planning to fail.
- When all's said and done a lot more is said than done.
- The more you plan the luckier you get.
- A project gets a year late one day at a time.
- Everyone asks for a strong project manager - when they get him they don't want them.
- If there is a 50% chance of something going wrong then 9 times out of 10 it will.
- You can tell a man is clever by his answers – you can tell a man is wise by his questions.

And a note of caution – understand clearly what is being asked of you:

A young project manager was leaving the office after a long day when he found the CEO standing in front of a shredder with a piece of paper in his hand.

'Listen' said the CEO 'This is a very sensitive and important document, and my secretary is not here. Can you make this thing work?'

'Certainly' said the young project manager in a confident tone. He turned on the machine, inserted the paper, and pressed the start button.

'Excellent, excellent' said the CEO as his paper disappeared inside the machine 'I just need the one copy'.

And now for something completely different[12]

I am grateful the community of project managers out there who were happy to share the following snippets of humour, I am quoting the contributors rather than any primary source.

A man walked into a pet shop and was looking at the animals on display. While he was there, another customer walked in and said to the shopkeeper, 'I'll have a C monkey please' The shopkeeper went over to a cage at the side of the shop and took out a monkey. He fitted a collar and lead on it and handed it to the customer, saying 'That'll be £2,000 please'.

The customer paid and walked out with his monkey.

Surprised at this the man went over to the shopkeeper and said 'That seems a lot of money for one monkey'. The shopkeeper replied 'Ah, well that monkey can program in C, it is very fast, tight code, no bugs, well worth the money'.

The man looked around the shop and spotted another monkey in another cage. He noted the price tag on the cage and cried out 'This one costs £5,000 what on earth can it do?'

'Oh yeas that one is great, it's a C++ monkey, it can manage object-oriented programming, Visual C++, and even some Java' said the shopkeeper proudly.

---

12   Well I had to get at least one Monty Python quote in here didn't I? 'And Now for Something Completely Different' was a catchphrase from the TV series and was also a film spin-off featuring favourite sketches from the first two seasons. The film, released in 1971, consists of 90 minutes of the best sketches seen in the first two series of the television show. The sketches were remade on film without an audience, and were intended for an American audience which had not yet seen the series. The announcer (John Cleese) uses the phrase several times during the film, in situations such as being roasted on a spit and lying on top of the desk in a small, pink bikini.

The man continued to look around and finally saw a third monkey in a cage all on its own. The price tag read a staggering £50,000. The man gasped to the shopkeeper 'That one costs more than all the others put together. What on earth does it do?'.

The shopkeeper replied 'Well, I haven't actually seen it do anything as yet but it says it's a project manager!'.

Stephen Carter

Some more project management laws that affect us all:

The more time you spend in reporting on what you are doing, the less time you have to do anything. Stability is achieved when you spend all your time doing nothing but reporting on the nothing you are doing – Cohn's law.

Attempts to get answers early in a project fail as there are many more wrong questions than right ones. Activity during the early stages should be dedicated to finding the correct questions. Once the correct questions have been identified correct answers will naturally fall out of subsequent work without grief or excitement and there will be understanding of what the project is meant to achieve – Hoggarth's law.

Russell Kemp

A new project manager spends a week at his new office with the project manager he is replacing. On the last day the departing project manager tells him 'I have left three numbered envelopes in the desk drawer. Open an envelope if you encounter a crisis you can't solve'.

Three months down the track there is a major drama, everything goes wrong, all the usual stuff, and the project manager feels very threatened by it all. He remembers the parting words of his predecessor and opens the first envelope. The message inside says 'Blame your predecessor' He does this and gets off the hook.

About half a year later, the project costs have rocketed combined with other serious issues. The project manager quickly opens the second envelope. The message read 'Replan', this he does and the project quickly rebounds.

Three months later, at his next crisis, he opens the third envelope. The message inside simply says 'Prepare three envelopes'.

Kate Thording

A lawyer, a doctor and a project manager were discussing the relative merits of having a wife or a mistress.

The lawyer says 'For sure a mistress is better. If you have a wife and want to divorce, there are a number of complex legal problems to resolve and it will probably be very expensive'.

The doctor says 'It's better to have a wife because the sense of security and wellbeing lowers your stress and your blood pressure and is good for your health'.

The project manager says 'You're both wrong. It's best to have both so that when your wife thinks you're with your mistress, and your mistress thinks you're with your wife then you can go to the office and get some work done'.

Colin Russell

Employer 'In this project we need someone who is responsible'.

Candidate 'I'm the one you want. On my last project, every time anything went wrong, they said I was responsible'.

Lynne Painter

The less you know about the project, the easier it is to generate fake estimates

Liam Dillon

Types of Project Manager
- If you get in my way, I'll kill you! – An ideal project manager
- If you get in my way, you'll kill me!–A somewhat less than ideal project manager
- If I get in my way, I'll kill you!–A slightly misguided project manager
- If I get in your way, I'll kill you! - A tough project manager
- If get kill in will way I you –A dyslexic, functionally illiterate project manager
- I am the way! Kill me if you can!–A messianic project manager
- Get away, I'll kill us all! – A suicidal project manager
- If you kill me, I'll get in your way–A thoughtful but ineffective project manager
- If I kill you, I'll get in your way –A project manager who has trouble dealing with the obvious
- I am quite confident that there is nothing in the way, so no one will get killed–A project manager who is about to get in big trouble
- If you kill me so what? If you get in my way, who cares?–A weak, uninspired, lacklustre project manager
- If I kill me, you'll get your way – A pragmatic project manager
- If we get in each other's' way, who will get killed? - An utterly confused manager
- Kill me; it's the only way - every project manager to date

Scott MacKenzie

And here is a joke that I first heard Frank Saladis tell when we co-presented in Sweden a while ago. Actually, since he was opening keynote and I was closing keynote, when he started telling this joke I thought that he was using the joke about the Genie and the three wishes from *The Lazy Project Manager* that I intended to use in my own presentation and I would have drop it. In fact it was different, and funny, just change the geography to suit your own situation.

A Project Manager was having a lunch time stroll along the beach, as you do, when they happened upon a small brass lamp lying on the sand. Eagerly he grabbed the lamp and rubbed it and, of course, as in every fairy tale, the giant genie appeared in a puff of magic smoke.

'I am the genie of the lamp' he proclaimed 'and I will grant you any wish, what is your command?'

'Well you know I am currently working on a pretty tough project with work in both North America and Europe' said the Project Manager 'And it is taking me huge amounts of time travelling to airports and gong through security, getting on and off planes, passing through border control, waiting for my luggage to appear and then getting through customs before hiring a car and driving to the office. It would be really great to have a road bridge that I just drive across.'

'Wow' said the Genie 'A road bridge. I can see your problem but that is a pretty big ask, even for me. Do you have any other wishes that we can consider?'

'Sure' replied the Project Manager 'Can you make it so that on every future project the customer understands what they want up front, never changes their mind and never expands the scope part of the way through the project?'

The Genie looked and the Project Manager for a while and then said 'So, how many lanes are you wanting on that road bridge?'

I used this one in my book *The Lazy Winner* but it wasn't a Project Manager on the story then, now it is.

A Project Manager was finally on vacation[13] and was standing at

---

13 Yes, even Project Managers occasionally get to take a break (when they are not talking to Genies).

the pier of a small South Pacific Island village when a small boat with just one fisherman docked.

Inside the small boat were several large grouper. The Project Manager complimented the Islander on the quality of his fish and asked how long it took to catch them.

The Islander replied 'Only a little while'.

The Project Manager considered for a while and then asked the fisherman why didn't he stay out longer and catch more fish?

The Islander said he had enough to support his family's immediate needs.

The Project Manager then thought some more before he asked: But what do you do with the rest of your time?

The fisherman said 'Well I sleep late, fish a little, play with my children, take a late afternoon nap with my wife, stroll into the village each evening where I sip rum and play guitar with my friends, I have a full and busy life'.

The Project Manager scoffed at this answer and said 'Well I am a professional man with a PMP and an MBA and many years of experience and I could help you'.

The fisherman looked puzzled and asked 'How could you help me?'

You should spend more time fishing and, with the proceeds, buy a bigger boat. Then with the proceeds from the bigger boat you could buy several boats. Eventually you would have a fleet of fishing boats. Instead of selling your catch to a middleman you would sell directly to the processor, eventually opening your own cannery. You would control the product, processing and distribution' declared the Project Manager and went on 'You would, of course, need to leave this small fishing village and move to America where you will run your expanding enterprise'.

The South Seas fisherman asked 'But, how long will this all take?'

To which the Project Manager replied 'Oh about 15 to 20 years should do it I think'

'What next' asked the man.

The Project Manager laughed and said that's the best part 'When the time is right you would announce an IPO and sell your company stock to the public and become very rich, you would make millions'.

'Millions, really? Then what?' Questioned the villager

The Project Manager said 'Then you would retire. Move to a small fishing village where you would sleep late, fish a little, play with your kids, take a late afternoon nap with your wife, stroll to the village in the evenings. Here you could sip rum and play your guitar with your friends'.

The fisherman smiled and picked up his catch and headed home.

6
PM Celebrity Gossip – 24 style: Kenny Phipps

I have, pretty much since series 1, been a 24^{14} fan and have been known to ask myself in time of desperation: 'What would Jack do?' Alas, the answer would – had I gone with the suggested action – resulted in me being arrested for numerous crimes.

However, there remain certain traits of 'Jack Bauer' that can – and should – be considered in managing projects. Now, I say all of this a little 'tongue in cheek', but am somewhat serious as well. Allow me to explain.

(In a deep voice) 'Previously on (Project) 24...'

At any given point; with the possible exception of the immediate beginning of the project ('day' in Jack's case) there should be an obvious sense of urgency across the project organisation; 'CTU' if you like.

The immediate needs are defined by those in the field (project team) and fed back to where they can efficiently be resourced, analysed and fulfilled (the PMO). Those in the field manage the relationship with those that are ultimately paying (with money in the case of customers for those on projects; and with their life for fugitives on the 'run') and filter through

---

14 Just in case you are one of the few who missed this, 24 was an American television series produced for the Fox network and syndicated worldwide, starring Kiefer Sutherland as Counter Terrorist Unit (CTU) agent Jack Bauer. Each 24-episode season covers 24 hours in the life of Bauer, using the real time method of narration

the volume of information that comes in; directing the useful information again to those that can efficiently process.

Talking of efficiency, when it came to 'meetings'; these would be replaced with 'interrogations' whereas to derive any and all missing information that was required for an effective delivery. Can you imagine the quality of any 'discovery' information that would come in if there were knee caps at risk? There would be little need for minutes as most points needing action would be more than clear. No need to note Actions; these would be hammered home at gunpoint!

In the event that good quality discovery information could not be obtained and while knee-cap bits are being mopped form the walls; a 'Plan B' would kick in. In executing (emphasis on the 'executing') Plan B; we would move straight to implementation given that it's better to do it than to talk about it – this saves time, money and effort.

A field unit would be mobilised for an en-mass hit. Taking up position on customers sites, where a military operation would disseminate user communications via loud speakers, not via email that some would inevitably 'not get, logoff and step away from the computer immediately'; this would reverberate around the immediate vicinity. Laptop and desktop would be replaced, cabled, powered and anyone caught moaning would be subject to Sensory Deprivation for 30 minutes; just after a quick dose of Sodium Thiopental (truth serum) to derive any and all passwords, mobile device inventory and 'essential file' locations.

Each desktop change would be exactly 7 mins; before the field unit would fall back in formation, removing old kit for secure disposal. Any VIPs that were knocked out to prevent 'stress' would be woken with smelling salts by their PAs and handed a brand new Blackberry.

This Project Approach would negate the need for extended user communication; reminders and 'I am sorry, I have a yoga class Friday, can we do it next month?', and save 2/3rds of implementation costs. Those, that in the space of 11.5 minutes since Tech Refresh, that have forgotten their passwords would be subject to a lobotomy and sent to make small toy cars in a remote island; due to being useless.

Given the lack of need for a delayed project start, a militarised planning phase, a condensed execution (and literal execution in extreme cases); and little need for VIP 'hyper-care', cost savings would be truly extensive. Run costs would be reduced as the useless people would have been disposed of. Remaining headcount would exude increased motivation due to the presence of an armed post-migration floor walker (ex-SAS or Navy Seal crazy with anger management problems) and productivity would be up.

Additional costs would be saved during implementation as the Military Field Unit used recruits in training with the only live ammo being held by the Senior Field Engineer to which Escalations (stupid people!) would be (fed) handed.

Jack would prepare highlighted reporting at the end of each implementation stage/gate (operation) outlining Build and Run metrics, any exceptions that occurred and the % of service improvements made (stupid people 'reassigned')

Lesson Learned would be short.

Very short.

Kenny Phipps, Professional Contractor of 16 years, owner of v6, a cloud platform for SMEs; co-owner of Team MEDD, Integration, Migration & Deployment Services for the Enterprise and an avid Jack Bauer fan.

'Follow your dreams. Just make sure to have fun too'

Chris Brown

7
Fun motivation

We all understand that a motivated project team is a productive project team but also there will be times, as a project manager, when you just have to step up that whole 'motivation' injection to overcome a particularly difficult time, either through a tough challenge or during a demanding period of effort or perhaps just when the team is going through some form of change or other.

What can you do at these critical times? Well here are some great ideas from some of your project management peers that might just inspire you when the time comes for you to become Mr or Mrs Motivator for your team.

Inspiration

One recent example of how I encouraged a cross-site agile team to come closer together was to set-up a weekly email called 'playlist of the week'. Everyone in the team (plus a few other people who found out about the weekly email and asked to be added) gets the email that I send on a weekly basis and they respond with a link to a YouTube song that they like. It's really helped break down some of the cultural barriers as one part of the team is based in the UK and the other in the Ukraine. I never thought that I would listen to so much Russian soft rock!

The email has had the effect of making people feel included and a way to express themselves without the awkwardness of a team building exercise where you have to share something too personal. It's also a good way of letting off steam at the end of the week in a fun way.

Simson Leigh

Here is one instance where we built some fun activities into our project.

I was heading up a large program for an eLearning company. There was an offshore team of about 150 developers, graphic artists and instructional designers and to get this huge team to perform was a huge challenge. Not only were they offshore, our onshore team was spread across four locations, the program had an aggressive deadline and morale was slipping.

In this environment I decided to lighten things up and purchased 200 hats - a different colour hat for each team - red for developers, green for graphic artists, blue for instructional designers and so on. We also shipped a huge box full of hats to the offshore team. This got them so psyched and excited, that they started sending us photos with the hats on and conversations started flowing, personal connections were made, and guess what? Productivity increased.

We had a great program release and we all celebrated it with our colourful hats on.

Samir Penkar

One time I took over a project that was very problematic. The project was behind schedule, only a little progress was done, and all of the resources were apparently 'trying to kill one another!'.

When I started to talk to the team, I realized that the project scope was not that complicated. It was a project to review the process base for software development of one of Brazil's largest software houses. The problem was that roles and responsibilities were not defined at the beginning, and this resulted in many conflicts during the execution.

Once I took over the project, I decided to establish some 'quick wins', a series of minor milestones that we would focus on to deliver in the first month; to show the client (and the project team) that the project was finally progressing.

I set a milestone for the first week and said to the group that I would 'bake a cake' and bring it to the office on Friday if the milestone was met. One of the resources laughed at my face (she was known to be a pretty good cook) and said I couldn't do it!

'If you can meet the milestone, I can bake a good cake!' I replied and the challenge was set.

What was a simple thing turned into a huge challenge! The team started to work hard just to see the project manager go to the kitchen and bake his own cake!

Well, at the end of the week, the milestone was successfully met, and I duly brought my homemade cake in to the office. It was not 'that' pretty but it was delicious! And even more delicious because we finally could advance with the project and get rid of those internal conflicts at the same time.

I have to say that the cake was pretty good too and the lady who said I could not bake a good cake asked me for the recipe and said it was delicious!

(What they didn't know was that I had baked another cake the day before just to test the recipe because I didn't want to fail in my challenge).[15]

Well, the next week I challenged our good cook to bring us a cake if we could meet the next milestone and it was done. With these simple activities I could relieve the tension, make the team change the focus from the conflicts to the project activities, and, from that moment on, things started to work out.

Oh, and I'm still enjoying going in to the kitchen but I need to confess that baking cakes is not my best skill!

Andre Choma

---

15   I think that they know now!

Team Spirit

At one of the major banks, the project team decided to decorate their office area with an Easter theme. Unsurprisingly this involved various daffodils, chicks and bunnies. But every morning on arrival at the office, the bunnies (and there were dozens of them) had been rearranged into compromising positions, doing what bunnies do best. We never found out who did it but were always keen to find out what our bunnies had been up to overnight!

Menna Pitts

A long time ago a software development team I was team leader for had an automated (UNIX) build script with test routines - this kind of thing is very common now but it wasn't then. Somehow during an earlier office refurbishment an old door handle managed to get left behind in the office.

Now one of the real issues we faced was when someone did some work that broke the automated build and test scripts. It was 'sort of' OK if your software failed but only if the rest of the build process ran through - a test could fail but not the testing process. I don't how first started but someone got awarded the door handle as 'knob of the week' and then it got passed on to the next person who broke the build and so on. It became a thing of pride as office visitors asked 'Why is there a door handle on your monitor?' the reply 'Oh I was knob of the week three weeks ago and I'm waiting to pass it on (I.e. I screwed up last but that was some time ago and since then we've all worked without getting wrong).

Simon Harris

My father in law was a project manager for years and one of his tools for team moral was the use of a 4 foot stuffed Scooby Doo! Whichever team member had had a set back or fluffed their job got the accolade of being 'Scoobied' for the day!

Everyone loved it!

Stephen Watkins

It's almost a no brainer when your successful projects have a common thread and that's team synergy. In our feeble attempts to gain this we run ourselves through the exercise of training, mentoring and coaching those that for good or bad are simply not a good fit in the team. Not always is this incompatibility driven by the lack of social skills, although developers are a quite fickle lot, but sometimes it simply a matter that they are not in a good place to be a cohesive element.

I remember one time, as we set out on a high pressure project which was quite common place, having not one but a small part of the team that seemed hell bent on doing their own thing. We tried what I thought was just about everything that was known at that time, even putting them on the hot seat to develop a portion of the system that no one else seemed to know how to address. They did it with flying colours and we gave them recognition, set them as examples of how to do hard things right and still no change. They chose to fly under their own agenda, stressing out each and every manager that had to interact with them. It wasn't that their conduct was particularly bad, and certainly not insubordinate, simply not sharing and often quite moody in terms of what they were working on and when.

Troubled as to what to do I remember clearly on a somewhat overcast day as I was passing through a small bazaar I noticed some old time trinkets out of the corner of my eye. On closer inspection the box contained maybe close to 100 mood rings, each one emitting a signal to me saying 'buy me', and so I did. I think it cost me a total of $10 as a left the market. My idea was to have some fun with the rings and see what comes as a result.

As I eagerly awaited the next scheduled meeting I pondered the question of what the reaction would be. On the fateful day as each person walked into the room, some with notebooks in hand, others with simply a coffee cup I awaited the 'problem children'. I opened the meeting with the agenda and then announced that before we got started we would need some help in getting off to a good start and we had to make sure that everyone's heart was in the project. As I scanned the room I could see eyes rolling and people trying to divert my stare. I passed out the rings and explained that as a team we needed to always be mindful of our moods as well as the moods of others, it's what you call being respectful I explained. If someone is having a bad day (black mood) then be especially nice and cooperative and if they are showing green look out because they might be a bit too romantic to remain in compliance with corporate policy. The room erupted in laughter as they compared their moods and joked about whether some would ever have a colour change in their ring or whether the colour being shown was reflecting multiple mood disorders.

I'm not sure if it was the rings or maybe just getting the issue out on the floor but from that day on the team seemed to function as one. When the project came to an end we really had a functioning team and not a dysfunctional family.

Jerry E. Durant

Our latest fun in our team was establishing 'Blondies' soccer team for intra-company sporting day[16].

It was a big success (3rd place in soccer competition nut with a 1st prize for team dress!) and we all enjoyed a big slice of fun. We have installed a wall of fame in our team space with pictures, diplomas, dress and medals - in order to remind us of this common fun experience. The positive impact for team spirit is quite remarkable.

Zdenek Vencl

---

16   I was provided a photograph of the 'Blondies' – but for your own safety and mental health it has been placed in the Appendices of this book – so you only have to view it by choice!

Some years ago I managed a large application development project for a software company – a new branch application for a major international betting company. We were supposed to replace the current system that was already obsolete and very inflexible. It was quite a challenge itself but also the team I got assigned never did anything so complex before and we all felt that it would not be easy.

The team members did not know each other very well and were not used to working together at all as the company just decided to start with the application development and therefore were recruiting new staff. Our project was in fact their first real project. But it was also a team of very clever analysts, programmers and testers who had a very high potential.

So my main task in the beginning of the project was to create a performing team and to convince everybody that our task was feasible and achievable. I introduced a rule –a penalty would have to be paid for being negative or pessimistic about the project (the money earned we would spent later in the pub of course). It really changed the atmosphere, the team learned to be optimistic and to have fun and whenever somebody expressed a pessimistic opinion regarding the project the others started to laugh and asked them to pay the fee immediately.

One day, when we came in the morning to the office, we found a short funny and very optimistic poem on the flipchart. It was about our application we were working on. It was along the lines that when released the application would be so successful that the other betting companies would have to close down. It was written by one colleague who was usually the first in the office.

Everybody liked it and it started something like a competition in poem writing and there was a new poem on the flipchart almost every day until we moved to a new office. We even learned the most popular ones by heart and were often quoting them. When we celebrated the end of the project we put the best poems on the walls of the pub.

The project itself was not easy at all. The client was really difficult and not cooperative and also the project was underestimated due to the company inexperience in the application development. However our perfect team overcame all the problems and the application was delivered and released to production successfully. The individual team members are now working for different companies but we still know about each other and meet whenever there is an opportunity (a new born child, Christmas, visit of a colleague working abroad, or simply 'we haven´t met for a long time'. It was the best team I ever worked with and we are all still remembered for the great atmosphere in the project and all of the fun we had.

Liba Vitackova

On a technical project to implement improved card security at one of the major banks, the design team were lamenting how the project senior team were so wooden. As a result we launched 'tree' day for the whole project team (around 50 people) without the knowledge of the senior leaders. Points were awarded for any mention of a tree, or wood related products that we could get into a meeting, minutes or other documentation. To this day, the business requirements documentation is scattered with numerous woody references.

Menna Pitts

Many years ago I was working on a highly pressurised project for a large investment bank. We were approaching year-end and our project just had to be delivered before the change freeze kicked in. No excuses! As a result we were working very long hours and tensions were rising.

As it happened, the yearly Christmas party was approaching, and back in those days the big companies really splashed out. For my team this was great news and perfect timing as we really needed a break. But little did we know that the party would also be a great team building event. As we arrived on the night we found that the company had organised a large fun fair for the party. As my team largely consisted of computer geeks and lads this was great news! We were nowhere to be seen at the dining table, but spent the entire evening in the bumper cars in our black ties and long evening dresses! What a sight! However crazy it sounds, this was the perfect opportunity for the team to bond. We got to let go of all the built-up tensions and laughed our way through it. I will never forget that night. We had so much fun as a team and it definitely increased our team spirit and morale in the months that followed.

Susanne Madsen

Reward and Recognition

As a way of building team spirit while 'giving back to the community we are invading for a few months', our traveling consultants save up the extra hotel amenities – soaps, shampoos, lotions, etc – and pick a local shelter to donate them to. Over the course of a few months, this adds up to a sizeable donation. Imagine if all traveling consultants did this!

Ted Nunn

I had a project manager who took the development team to lunch one day after a release and told them 'not to come back for the rest of the day'. It was a great piece of motivation, superb communication and made up for many hours of unpaid overtime worked as the team prepared for the release.

Mathew Strawbridge

We have had several Team celebrations at Center Parcs[17] where we enjoyed the swimming in the tropical paradise and other activities, at the pub and out for a Chinese meal ...

John Bridges

Small successes are always celebrated with the Danish Kaj cakes, these taste delicious and look like 'frogs' – yummy marzipan with a tasty filling inside. A real treat!

Finn Svenning

I was working on a project to implement redundant architecture for business continuity/disaster recovery. The Security/Risk SME on the project always built the requirements as if Olympia (State Capital and home to all state servers) were to become a 'smoking hole'. Actually he took this a bit too far in that he would not agree to any requirements that aligned with more likely scenarios such as fire in the data center, but that is beside the point. At the post project celebration I made 'smoking hole punch' - Rootbeer and ice cream in a punch bowl with lots of dry ice so it was really 'smoking'.

It got good laughs all round.

Vicki James

Marketing

One of my favourite project memories is the fun some people had with 'subversive' posters.

This was a large project, and we created PAMs overseas and shipped them over, dropped them into place (to simplify). PAM

---

17 Center Parcs is a European network of holiday villages incorporating a UK-based company, Center Parcs UK, which runs holiday villages in the United Kingdom and a sister enterprise, Center Parcs Europe, that operates in numerous locations in continental Europe.

stands for Pre-Assembled Module. You can imagine the fun the teams had when we went to Super PAMs... or SPAMs.... several PAMs joined together prior to transporting.

The real chuckle was the poster that appeared overnight all over the project offices with a can of SPAM cleverly 'photoshopped' onto one of our big movers with straps and all (safety of course!). The management weren't overly happy about it, but it was actually great PR for what we were doing.

As the manager of the QA engineering team, it gave us a fun opening to some painful meetings!

Becky Paroz

Bonding

We did one thing in a project which in a very simple way turned out as a success, a good conversation piece and something that (good or bad) marked us as mildly and harmlessly eccentric.

The scene is a Scrum project that had been going on for about 1½ years and nearing completion. Good and strong culture within the project team but some oncoming fatigue as we were distributed in the building and only had the coffee machine and the daily Scrum meeting as common meeting points. Relationship with the customer was basically OK but again, the project had been going on for some time and there were stakeholders outside the project where some welcomed what we did and others that wanted something else.

We needed something silly to gather around. Something which wasn't work related at all.

At one of the daily Scrums I suggested an antquarium and the team immediately grasped its immense value and usefulness. It's like an aquarium but for ants with a blue and nutritious gel where you put the ants and they live happily (?) for up to 6 months building ducts and moving dead comrades to the surface. The retailer claims the gel has been developed by NASA and on the rather elegant box we got it said that the antquarium was Version 2.0 with internet access and a practical jar to fetch ants with and a magnifying glass to find them not to mention the wooden stick for chasing ants into the jar.

The next step was to go on an ant chase and the team spent the one lunch chasing smaller and larger ants. It's quite tricky really. You only need ~20 ants in the little jar, but they are escape artists. (Eventually we learned that the best thing to do is simply open the little jar and put it in the ant trail. First we followed the instructions using the wooden stick and had ants everywhere; mostly up our sleeves, in our underwear and pockets.)

Our first mistake was to mix ants from different tribes – they successfully and swiftly killed each other. Chasing for a new population we finally found small black ants from the same tribe and put them in the antquarium. The antquarium was first placed in the room where PM resided and the room quickly became known as the 'ant farm' because of the diligent and industrious work that took place. The word spread and now the customer (also our adversaries) started to visit. We had many chats about things that were not politically inflamed and gained mutual respect and acceptance.

Of course the antquarium had to move to the other people in the team and wherever it went people talked about it, nursed the ants and buried the dead[18] (ants).

To cut a long story short – the project was delivered on time, the customer was happy (we believe also the adversaries) and all the ants are now dead. This was of course not the thing that made us deliver but it contributed in a small and silly way to the

---

18 I would love to say that no ants were harmed in the making of this project but clearly that would be a lie – so let's settle with they all lived full and happy lives and died peacefully in their sleep (except the ones that were killed in a vicious bloody fight with other ants of course).

climate in the project (and at £15 the money was extremely well spent).

Paul Leffler

Negotiation

I was lucky recently in being able to fly business class on an impressive airline. It was a very enjoyable experience (as far as flying is concerned) but I encountered one of the most intriguing pieces of negotiation I have ever come across.

Now on this airline the business class was fantastic, really comfortable full bed seats, loads of space, iPad style remote control, large TV screen, great food and drink, superb service etc. No complaints from me at all. But there was also a first class service – you never saw these travellers as they entered the airline separately and were kept well away from the rest of us mere mortals so you could only imagine the comfort and luxury that was afforded to them.

The flight I was on required a stop and when I re-boarded some of the passengers had changed. In the row next to me there was now a couple. They settled in and accepted a glass of champagne each and then one of the stewards came up to the man and spoke to him quietly. His face lit up and he turned to his partner and said 'They have offered me an upgrade to first class'.

His female companion took a sip from her glass and said – nothing.

He went on 'I have never been in first class before' and there was a sad desperate tone to his voice now.

The lady drank some more of her champagne and said – nothing.

He added 'I might never get to go in first class again …' the statement hung in the air as he looked at her imploringly, desperate for some form of approval to take this 'once in a lifetime opportunity' but she said – nothing.

After a few moments where you could almost hear his thought processes, certainly louder that the silence of the lady companion, he went up to the steward and spoke to him.

Now his options seemed to me to be a) be a saint and give the upgrade to his partner and stay in business class himself b) accept the upgrade himself and suffer the consequences of abandoning his partner in the lower grade cabin or c) reject the upgrade and stay with his partner. What would you do in this situation do you think?

What he did in fact was accept the upgrade but he actually spent more of his time back in business class, his seat was left empty, making sure that the lady was happy. I guess this way he got to see and experience first class a little, and tell his friends and colleagues about it, but also kept his relationship alive and well.

And the lady?

Well she enjoyed a number of glasses of champagne during the flight and I caught her smiling to herself each time he left her to take another few minutes in his first class cabin.

Peter Taylor

A warning

They say you can't have too much of anything but that is not necessarily true:

Beware of flip chart pen intoxication!

During what myself, and two Programme Managers referred to as a 'mega' planning session at the very start of plotting out the various projects in an organisational transformation programme, we locked ourselves away with plenty of brown paper, flip charts and the all essential post it's.

By the end of a productive day we would invite in our SRO[19] to give an update on where our combined genius had taken us as our planning started to take shape. On one memorable occasion, when we had found ourselves in a smaller than usual 'cupboard' and had decorated pretty much every wall with colourful flip charts (we had really gone to town) the SRO turned up to find us in tears with hysterical laughter and barely able to string a sentence together. After trying really hard yet unsuccessfully to 'get it' her face changed ...and with a very concerned look she noted the incredible level of 'fumes' in the air...a by-product of the nice new flip chart pens we had received that same morning.

No doubt about it, we were suffering from flip chart pen intoxication....a definite occupational hazard (although it made for some very interesting ideas which we had to reconsider slightly the next morning!)

Emma Peleshok

---

19 Senior Responsible Owner, in Office of Government Commerce terminology in the UK, is the individual responsible for ensuring that a project or programme of change meets its objectives

8
PM Celebrity Gossip – The bad parrot: Alfonso Bucero

John, a project manager, received a parrot as a gift. The parrot had a bad attitude and an even worse vocabulary.

Every word out of the bird's mouth was rude, obnoxious and laced with profanity. John tried and tried to change the bird's attitude by consistently saying only polite words, playing soft music and anything else he could think of to 'clean up' the bird's vocabulary.

Finally, John was fed up and he yelled at the parrot. The parrot yelled back. John shook the parrot and the parrot got angrier and even ruder. John, in desperation, threw up his hand, grabbed the bird and put him in the freezer. For a few minutes the parrot squawked and kicked and screamed.

Then suddenly there was total quiet. Not a peep was heard for over a minute.

Fearing that he'd hurt the parrot, John quickly open the door to the freezer. The parrot calmly stepped out onto John's outstretched arms and said 'I believe I may have offended you with my rude language and actions. I'm sincerely remorseful for my inappropriate transgressions and I fully intend to do everything I can to correct my rude and unforgivable behaviour.'

John was stunned at the change in the bird's attitude.

As he was about to ask the parrot what had made such a dramatic change in his behaviour, the bird spoke-up, very softly, 'May I ask what the turkey did?'

Many times I have come across team members who had a very negative attitude and but they changed eventually based on some bad consequences of their attitude.

Please never be a bad parrot.

Alfonso Bucero, MSc, PMP, PMI Fellow, is now an independent project management consultant and speaker. He is founder, partner and director of BUCERO PM Consulting in Spain. Bucero has a M.S. in computer science engineering. He is the author of five project management books and manages projects internationally.

9
Fun Status

One of my favourite words to update anyone on a project status is 'ticketyboo'.

Use it and I will guarantee that you will stop them in their tracks and most likely start a conversation that will be entertaining and enjoyable.

But what does it mean?

Well there are a number of theories regarding the origin of the expression but in general terms is 'all in order, satisfactory, as it should be' or 'Everything is going fine and things are proceeding smoothly or quickly'.

It first appeared in the early 1920s and was in general use by the 1940s. It is still used in the UK by people of 'a certain age' apparently and has become rather old fashioned (well that puts me in my place doesn't it).

There is one theory that it is a relic of the British Colonial presence in India and it may have originated in the British military with one of the most accepted and common theories connects it to the Hindi expression 'Tikai babu' or 'Tickee babu' meaning 'Everything's alright, sir'.

It could also be the combination of the phrase (favoured by toffs) of 'that's the ticket' with the childish phrase of 'peek-a-boo'.

There are others who believe that the expression may have originated in Scotland, where it's the title of a popular children's song. In fact a song called 'Everything Is Tickety-

Boo' was recorded by Danny Kaye[20] way back in 1958 as part of the film 'Merry Andrew'.

I have also been told that this expression is heard more often in Canada these days, but I can't confirm this at all except that as the term was popular in the RAF, and there were many Canadians working with the RAF during the war then the adoption of the term would make sense.

Regardless of origin and regardless of historical meaning I still maintain that it is one great word to sum up your project (hopefully) and one brilliant word to get people talking to you, and talking about the project as well.

If you have a word in your own language[21] that maybe offers a similar answer to the question 'how is the project?' then why not share it with me at peter.b.taylor@btinternet.com or through LinkedIn or Twitter?

In the meantime I give you 'ticketyboo' – use it today, why not?

You will find yourself totally 'ticketyboo'.

---

20 Feel free to look this up on YouTube and have fun learning the lyrics at your next project team meeting.

21 Sorry my lovely North American friends but I am absolutely excluding that over-used word 'awesome' as far as this is concerned, I am sure you have better words than this one.

10
PM Celebrity Gossip – The asterisk on projects: Jeff Furman

Homerun king Roger Maris[22] never actually was given that much talked-about asterisk in the record books. But the idea of an asterisk tacked-on to an achievement lives on.

The biggest project I ever completed was bringing an IT Change Management System in a large NY brokerage to almost* 100% utilization. I say 'almost*' because ... well let me explain.

My team and I were tasked with implementing a system that had been mandated by our CIO for use by the department's 1,000+ developers for managing their code changes. At that time, more than a year after the mandate, almost none of the developers had migrated to the system – this was primarily due to the department's lack of guns to hold against their heads; that is there was no compelling reason for them to make the change.

With a combination of service, charm, and mainly training, we ultimately convinced the developers that the system was indeed in their best interest. And to the CIO's amazement,

---

22 Roger Maris was an American baseball right fielder who played 12 seasons in Major League Baseball (MLB) on four teams, from 1957 through 1968. Maris hit a record 61 home runs during the 1961 season for the New York Yankees, breaking Babe Ruth's single-season record of 60 home runs in 1927. Maris' record stood for the next 37 years.

we achieved what came to be referred to as 100% compliance.

But there was one notable exception: a high-powered, Wall Street-suspendered holdout, who maintained that his system was 'too unique and important to risk being put under change control'.

As a result he never let his people use the full CM system (and worse, he got us to customize a scaled-down access just for his group, so he could say he was compliant*.

So here's to you, Jean-Pierre (not real-name name) for protecting your perfect* applications from the department's standard, and for giving your 110%*!

Jeff Furman, PMP® is a Project Management Instructor and the author of The PM Answer Book. Contact him at Jeff@Jeff-Furman. com or www.Jeff-Furman.com and find more about his book at www. PMAnswerBook.com

'A day without laughter is a day wasted'

Charlie Chaplin

11
Fun ideas

Communication of ideas

You can easily use fun to get across some more challenging ideas. Here is an example I used to explain Expectation Management.

The wheels touched down and seconds later there was a loud fanfare.

'Another on time arrival ...' was the proud declaration '... last year over 90% of our flights arrived on time ...'

I had just been to Sweden; Gothenburg to be exact, a very nice city as it happens and one I would recommend a visit to if you ever get the chance.

Anyway, I was on one of those low cost airlines where the general accent of the crew is Irish.

We were in fact 20 minutes 'early' on the home flight and on the way out we were 25 mins 'early' – I say 'early' because firstly arrival in airline terms means the time at which you touch down versus actually arriving somewhere useful and where you can leave the plane without getting arrested. And secondly I am somewhat suspicious that maybe, just maybe, there was so much contingency added to the flight times that arriving 'early' was all but guaranteed. That said, if this was true then that makes the 10% of flights that were reported late even worse than they officially are.

Imagine if you declared that your IT solution project was fully finished and ready for users to get their grubby hands on but that it was actually hidden away on a backup server and it would be another week before the customer could use it properly?

Imagine if you built so much contingency in to your project plan that you added 25% to the cost but you still had a track record that showed that you managed projects that ran way over schedule– do you think that would be acceptable?

It all reminds me of a story I was told some time ago. An American low cost airline ran a customer survey, as they often do, to see how happy their customers were. From this survey the number one issue raised was that it took a long time for the checked in baggage to arrive on the carousel.

The airline came up with a truly novel solution to this. Baggage handling is slightly out an airlines control and so this particular airline rather than addressing the problem through the baggage handling side addressed the problem by requesting the landing gates furthest from the baggage hall.

The result was twofold: They saved a little money by using these less popular gates and secondly passengers ignored the time that it took to leave the plane and walk all the way from the far gates to the baggage hall but instead were delighted to see their bags waiting for them on the carousel thereby causing them no waiting time.

The airline had not addressed the problem per se but had made their customers perception of their overall service increase as future surveys proved.

Expectation management is critical to all projects so get that feedback throughout your project lifecycle and react accordingly; sometimes you just may have to get creative.

Here's another one that you can use to demonstrate the need to fully understand and fully train people in testing methods perhaps, or just plain getting communication right. Now there are many stories about this out there in Google land and I have no idea if they are true or not, it doesn't matter, it is a great story whatever version you read.

Scientists at NASA had developed a gun for the purpose of launching dead chickens. It is used to shoot a dead chicken at the windshield of airline jet, military jet, or the space shuttle, and at that vehicles maximum travelling velocity. The idea being that it would simulate the frequent incidents of collisions with airborne fowl and therefore determine if the windshields are strong enough to endure high-speed bird strikes.

Good idea.

British engineers, upon hearing of the gun, were eager to test it on the windshields of their new high-speed trains. However, upon firing the gun, the engineers watched in shock as the chicken shattered the windshield, smashed through the control console, snapped the engineers' backrest in two, and embedded itself into the back wall of the cabin.

Horrified and puzzled the engineers sent NASA the results of the experiment, along with the designs of the windshield and asked the NASA scientists for any suggestions.

A very short while later the NASA scientists sent back to the British engineers a brief response.

Thaw the chicken!

And this one is from *The Lazy Project Manager and the Project from Hell* that I love using in presentations (about presentations).

I was recently in a restaurant in a foreign land (well foreign to me of course but less so to the locals).

The location was good, the décor and ambience very acceptable, the company most enjoyable, and the snow fell softly outside providing a winter wonderland visual delight through the large windows.

But sadly all of that positive build-up for a great evening's dining was almost outweighed by the food and service.

After an initial ordering experience the diners elected to eat the same main course but each agreed that the chef's vegetable of choice for the evening was not to their personal liking. It was the humble Brussels sprout, a member of the brassica family that enjoys a somewhat tarnished image which, considering its status as a nutritional power-house, is perhaps a little unfair. Its reputation is perhaps mostly due to the great British Christmas Day cooking technique: take sprouts, cut, trim, boil until at least twice dead and then for five minutes more. Then, finally, pile into a large dish and leave – because nobody actually likes Brussels sprouts (at least not cooked this way).

Anyway the request was made to replace said evil vegetable with an alternative, and asparagus tips were requested. And so the meal continued through a mediocre appetizer and on until the main course finally arrived ... without Brussels sprouts (the good news) but also without anything in their place as requested (the bad news).

The waiter was recalled and cajoled and encouraged to resolve this rapidly, at which the staff applied all of their skills and training, by ignoring us and disappearing. Eventually after a long period, during which most of the meal was consumed, the waiter did reappear and proceeded to almost, but not quite, save the entire situation.

With a silver platter and a silver fork of delicate proportions the waiter proceeded to ceremoniously, and with great flourish, place two small asparagus tips across the centre of each diner's remaining half-eaten meal.

It was theatrical and exaggerated and, had it not been for the sheer humour of the whole thing, he may just have got away with it. Presentation can win the day.

There is an old story about a crisis in a company when it

was discovered that one of their products was actually killing customers. This was a major issue and one that delivered headlines that were very bad news for the company. However a savvy and spirited marketing executive quickly went to work to resolve the situation. After a few days of bad publicity and press, with the death toll mounting, the marketeer launched a major fight back.

The first press release read 'Company X extremely concerned for its customers...'

Sadly the problems continued and more customers met their maker as a result of the killer products. The bad publicity continued and the situation looked desperate.

The marketing executive did not walk away from the challenge nor did he give up the battle. He worked late into the night thinking blue sky thoughts about a solution to this issue and finally came up with a plan.

The next day a press release was delivered to the world at large that simply read 'Company X sees a massive reduction in dissatisfied customers...'

It is all in the presentation and in turning negatives in to positives.

Our waiter tried but just failed; he couldn't carry it off completely and is probably from Barcelona anyway (yes that is a Fawlty Towers[23] reference and not an insult to wonderful Barcelona, one of my favorite cities).

---

23 Fawlty Towers is a British sitcom produced by BBC Television and first broadcast on BBC2 in 1975. Twelve episodes were made. The show was written by John Cleese and his then wife Connie Booth, both of whom also starred in the show. The series is set in Fawlty Towers, a fictional hotel in the seaside town of Torquay, on the 'English Riviera'. The plots centre around tense, rude and put-upon owner Basil Fawlty (Cleese), his bossy wife Sybil, a comparatively normal chambermaid Polly, and hapless Spanish waiter Manuel (who is from Barcelona) and their attempts to run the hotel amidst farcical situations and an array of demanding and eccentric guests. In a list drawn up by the British Film Institute in 2000, voted by industry professionals, Fawlty Towers was named the best British television series of all time

As a project manager you have to be calm, confident, assured and in control at all times. There will be times when you need to recover from sticky situations and on those occasions you need to have the skill to find the positive and the will to present it convincingly.

Presentation counts.

And do make sure that when you communicate as a project manager you communicate well. Here is a cautionary tale about invoking perhaps the wrong sort of fun in to a project meeting.

Good project managers know that a successful project meeting starts with a clear agenda and a strict time management for each topic. That is necessary but not enough. Any interruption during the meeting could destroy any agenda and time schedule.

For instance, when I was coordinating a collaboration project meeting in Panama with a team of 50 members, 10 minutes before the meeting I decided to go to the restroom. When I came back to kick-off the meeting just in time to start the meeting, everybody was on the floor laughing loudly.

Why? Well I forgot to disconnect my wireless microphone when I was away and everybody was hearing what I was up to through the speakers.

Conclusion: It is pretty good to open a meeting with a funny story to break the ice. However, it is perhaps much better if you don´t use this kind of introduction to a meeting.

Pablo Lledó

I totally concur with this advice having also been on a conference call when one member decided it was time for a 'comfort break' and, yes, forgot to switch off their headset, or at least put it on mute.

My biggest laugh of the year came in a conversation with someone who was in charge of project manager training for a large corporation. He said (referring to exposing PMs to new methods and practices):

'You can lead a horse to water, but you can't make him drink the Kool-Aid'

He was quite serious (I won't say 'dead serious') so I couldn't laugh until after I'd hung up the phone, which was tough!

Jeannette Cabanis-Brewin

And when comes to progress updates it is definitely all about asking the right question.

'Hi! What is the status of your project? Is progress being made?
'Hi! Not much at the moment...'
'Could you be more specific than that?'
'Absolutely nothing'

Nikolay Shvedchikov

Think also about the challenge of language (and culture of course) when working with global teams.

I was in a brainstorming session with a big group of Indian developers for one of my key projects. We were in the midst of a heated up debate and I ended my argument with a sentence – '... In the end, it's always wrong.' I wasn't sure if it was due to my accent or I was speaking too fast, but what I did realize was the facial expressions on some of the Indian developers changed drastically. I could sense that they weren't very happy, but I just couldn't tell why. I was told by one of them later that I shouldn't be so rude to say 'Indian is always wrong.' OMG... I got a hit on the head and realized what mistake I had made. It seems like when I uttered the three words 'In the end' very quickly, they do sound

like 'Indian' and that was the root cause of the misunderstanding.
Wai Mun Koo

Actually Wai Mun Koo offered me another piece of insight not related directly to communication but worth sharing.

There was once a colleague who told me that he believed that Sir Isaac Newton was a great project manager. I asked him why. He explained it with Newton's second law that leads to the formula $f = m \times a$, in which he stated that the ingenuity of this formula helped him to understand a very intriguing relationship in project management where resistance force (from the end users) equals to the madness multiplied by the aggravation. I hope Newton won't jump up from his grave when he hears that.

To conclude the communications theme let me share with you one story I was told some time ago but a wily clever project manager.

The challenge they were facing was getting access to a senior product development manager who was not returning calls, replying to email etc and yet was a key person this project manager needed to have a conversation with regarding some product related issues with their project.

After trying many traditional approaches this project manager came up with a radical an alternative idea. They had learnt that the product team met once a week after working hours to talk about planned product developments, socialise and eat pizza.

This project manager spotted their opportunity and intercepted the pizza delivery guy and stuck on the pizza boxes messages that went along the line of 'I urgently need to speak with you – call me'.

Guess what? Within ten minutes the product development

manager was on the phone to the project manager and a good conversation ensued.

So don't be afraid to think outside that box occasionally.

Team spirit

Fun really has a good home when it comes to team building, bonding and just generally making sure the spirits stay up – even during those low project points.

I was working on a project many years ago and it was one of those projects that reached a very low point when no progress was being made, well no real progress anyway, and everybody was blaming everybody else about whose fault it was. Team members were turning against other team members and the atmosphere was not good at all. If you have ever experienced a project like this you will understand what I am saying, and if you haven't them long may that continue and just accept my work that it is not a nice place to be.

I had tried many things but nothing seemed to be working. In the end I took the decision to take the core team off site to a local hotel where we tried some (re) team building and some 'blue sky' thinking and all that jazz.

It still wasn't working by the afternoon and so, in a moment of desperation, I stood up and said to everyone that I was going to solve all of the problems on this project right now.

That got their attention I must say.

I walked out of the room we were in, closed the door and (in a very loud voice) pretended to be my boss firing me. After a few moments I walked back in to the room and most people got the joke –one or two did look disappointed that I was still employed but that is life I guess.

Honestly I do believe that mad fun act just broke the ice,

eased the tension and broke some barriers down that had recently built up between people and from that point we slowly and painfully got the project back up and running. It was no shining example of project perfection still, it was late, reduced in scope, and way over budget but it did deliver some of the business benefits expected of it.

Humour helped save the day in this case.

Team discipline

Not an area that you might think fun can be used but you are wrong as we can hear from one person.

I thought you might be interested to know how I handle a scenario with individuals/teams not delivering to the time/quality/cost expected in a light-hearted way. In this situation I treat them like my 4 year old daughter in that they get told they'll be put on the 'naughty step'. If things don't improve then the threat is executed and they are put onto the naughty step – this involves being monitored more closely (regular update meetings, no stone left unturned etc) until a point where they've 'been good' (i.e. can be trusted to deliver again) and can come off it. It's a great way of making the message clear but maintaining good relationships.

I am sure there are more tips that can be used from the 'Supernanny[24]' series of books.

Kitty Mann

---

24 Supernanny is a reality TV programme which originated in the UK about parents struggling with their children's behaviour. The UK version has aired on Channel 4 with E4 showing repeats since 2004. The show features professional nanny Jo Frost, who devotes each episode to helping a family where the parents are struggling with their child-rearing. Through instruction and observation, she shows the parents alternative ways to discipline their children and regain order in their households. Frost is a proponent of the 'naughty chair' theory of discipline and is strictly opposed to spanking. Its competing series was Nanny 911 in the U.S., it

I am guessing Kitty is not a person to be messed with and that Christmas is a time when all of her team members are on their very best behaviour ... she knows when you've been naughty and she knows when you've been nice.

Team direction

I definitely like this tale of project effort and the application of time in an inappropriate way. I often talk about 'reporting is not communicating' and it can also be said that too many meetings isn't about communicating, or making any real progress either.

Three months in (i.e. post honeymoon period) a software development project of mine hit a major snag. My technical architect Hugh declared our proposed solution infeasible. Not 'It'll take a bit more time and money than we thought' but 'we can't implement the software we've chosen.'

The proposal described two pieces of software seamlessly integrating to unlock a wealth of features and benefits. But we neither owned nor had any particular familiarity with the software in question.

My first action was to escalate. Senior management needed to be informed and let's be honest, there's comfort in sharing a problem, (We term this the 'Marmite[25] strategy: not because you love/hate it, but because it's important to spread the blame thinly and evenly.)

---

aired on ABC and Style Network. there is a Supernanny USA as well, also with Jo

25 Marmite is the brand name for a food spread made from yeast extract, a by-product of beer brewing. The British version of the product is a sticky, dark brown paste with a distinctive, powerful flavour, which is extremely salty. This distinctive taste is reflected in the British company's marketing slogan: 'Love it or hate it'.

The result was the appointment of Max -- a grizzled project troubleshooter. Max instituted a daily 09:00 'all-hands' team meeting to review progress and set corrective actions. We drew up contingency plans and developed strategies. Much activity ensued although unfortunately none of it helped with the fundamental problem.

So Max upped the pace and our lives became a blur of technical option workshops.

The crunch came at the end of the third week. The all-hands briefing took two hours to tortuously review the bloated actions log, finishing just in time for another technical options workshop. This over-ran, leaving us to squabble over the small plate of custard creams in lieu of the usual bacon sarnie[26] from the canteen. At 1505 Max announced, 'Let's pick this up another time. I'm late for my next meeting.'

'Not really' I said. 'Next up is the afternoon checkpoint and everyone's already in this meeting', thus we moved swiftly and seamlessly into the third meeting of the day.

'Right' said Max briskly 'Update me on progress'.

What did he expect? We had been in wall-to-wall meetings since the previous progress report at 09:00, ergo nobody had even been back to their desks. It was a pattern that more or less summed up the last three weeks of intensive navel gazing.

Max frowned deeply, causing a series of wrinkles to march up his forehead, lending him more than a passing resemblance to a Klingon.

'I'm very unhappy about this lack of progress. You're not keeping to plan. Until I get to the bottom of why no progress is being made, I'm convening twice daily progress reviews for the entire team.'

We did the only decent thing we could... we laughed.

Shortly afterwards, Hugh came down with a nasty bout of

---

26   British slang for 'sandwich'.

stress-induced flu, which laid him low for a week. Just what we needed, you might think. As it turned out, it was.

After a day or two, he felt well enough to do a bit of technical reading. He lay in bed mulling things over while knocking back various flu remedies. He returned to work with the answer, a cunning technical work-around that none of the software vendors had even realised was possible. It was enough to kick-start the project and for us to finally shake off 'Mad' Max.

And the lesson? Well you can run as hard as you like up the wrong escalator, lots of effort but no tangible progress. Or you can let it carry you to the bottom and look for an up-escalator to take you where you want to go.

Tutus Manus

But as ever a word of caution, be humorous but be careful as well:

Many, many years ago I assumed the project management role for a global ERP[27] deployment and was both proud and excited about this opportunity.

The customer company was based out in Sweden and there was a Steering Meeting coming up and so I threw myself into energetic preparation for this all important meeting. Representatives from around the world were flying in to sanction the ramp-up of the project and this would be my first time in the spotlight and I so wanted to make the right impression naturally.

When we arrived for the two days of meetings I was rather nervous but settled in to the pre-Steering Meeting sessions and engaged in both business and social interactions. By the time

---

27 Enterprise resource planning (ERP) systems integrate internal and external management of information across an entire organization—embracing finance/accounting, manufacturing, sales and service, customer relationship management, etc. ERP systems automate this activity with an integrated software application.

of the second day and that big meeting with the CEO of the company I was feeling on top of my game.

By the time it came to my formal presentation I was buzzing – things were going well, this was going to be great.

The room was large and at one end was a massive white screen for the overhead projector. Behind this was an equally massive whiteboard (this is an important point to remember in my later defence).

The discussion had reached a point of agreeing the levels of standardisation of date around the world. Part numbers and descriptions common and standard, bills of material, standard but other data was less clear. I was displaying a graph of the standardisation curve on the screen when the CEO stopped the conversation and said that, as I was the expert in these matters, what was my opinion on where they should aim to be?

I took up the black marker pen from the table, swung round to the screen and, as I summarised what I considered best practice, placed to strokes of the pen on the white background to form an 'x marks the spot'.

'I believe you should aspire to this level of global standardisation' I proudly declared and then stood watching the black cross moving to and fro … I had placed my declaration in bold style on the beautiful white projection screen.

After a short pause, when I had everyone's attention the CEO said dryly 'Well I guess we won't forget that will we…'

And 'we' didn't as it was always on that screen each and every Steering Meeting I attended after that day.

12
PM Celebrity Gossip – It's the end of the world: Jon Quigley

It was a forgotten western outpost of a large global company. The personnel were few, the scope of the work great. The goal was to bring a new embedded control unit to the vehicle. This is a project within a global organization, with local (regional) execution required to deliver the final instantiation of the product. The local deliveries are to address the specific functions and features for the products, each site delivering a set of functions to meet the local markets.

The other parts of the company have much more human resources available to them to do the work. At this site, the development has been typically outsourced to the larger sites, with the product integrated at this local site. However, for this project the North American site will sit at the big boy table. To elaborate, at Thanksgiving or other large American holiday, you would often see the entire family celebrating the holiday in one house. The dining room table would not be large enough for all family members to sit. The family would put together smaller tables at which the children would sit for the meal. The adults sit at the larger table and will periodically go to the small tables and make sure the younger folks are okay, that they do not want for food or drink. Previous development work was handled in the larger European organizations, but the point behind this project was to make it possible for the individual geographic regions to develop the product, to make it possible to alter the product quickly for their specific customers. Untangled by the other global product development effort, the product is more quickly adapted to the locale. This was a new way of working, and a new level of responsibility for the North American organization.

Since this was a new way of working, the available resources with the requisite skill were few and their capability was untried. The most probable people with the skill and drive to ensure success were selected. They were then co-located in a specific room and assigned areas of responsibility. The scant resources and the need for a very productive team, meant the typical way of managing a project would not likely yield success. The team worked into a method that can be described in retrospect as proto-scrum. Communication was prized over formal risk management and long term project time plans. The product requirements were delivered just in time for the product development. The product software contents and build were just in time for testing. This was done, not so much as a conscious method, or management philosophy but due to the logistics of minimal available resources applied where needed when needed.

The entire situation seemed a daunting task, and to highlight that point there was considerable dark humor around the work as the team went about the task of developing and delivering the product. The team consisted of people who were not overly optimistic and could readily see the trouble areas and knew the probability of success was far from certain. There would be no way of sugar coating with a bunch of management speaking about challenges (instead of problems). The people were generally positive minded and aggressive toward solving problems, but there was an underlying tone of doom and sarcasm. For example, Gary Owen was frequently whistled in the room and hallways where this group worked. For those of you unfamiliar with US history, Gary Owen is associated with Custer's Cavalry, and that did not end too well for Custer and his men in the hills of Montana. Frequently, under the most trying of times in the project, the group resorted to the REM song 'It's the End of the World'.

The individuals, including Michael McKinley, Wesley Chominsky and Subramanian Arumugamknew, knew what was at stake was the growth and reputation of the local site. This local site was previously a following site, a dependent site. It was a site in which the embedded technical competence was perceived by the rest of the global organization, to be scant or even deficient. The effort was not to give birth to a new product, but to invigorate the local site with the perspective of being equal to the rest of the globe in spite of the fewer numbers. At stake was the promise of sitting at the same table as the rest of the global development organization, of being more of a partner and less of a dependent.

Jon M Quigley is a teacher, speaker, writer and intellectual property generator. He has an Electronics Engineering Degree, an MBA in Marketing and a Master's of Science in Project Management. He holds PMP certification from PMI, and has won the Volvo Technology Award and the 3P Technical Award. He has co-authored 7 books all of which are project management, product development and software centric. Additionally, he has generated 7 US patents over his more than 20 years. Jon is also on the Western Carolina University Masters in Project Management Curriculum Advisory Board as well as the Forsyth Technical Community College Business Administration (Project Management) Advisory Committee. He is the co-founder of Value Transformation LLC a business training organization (www.valuetransform.com) and can be contacted at Jon.Quigley@valuetransform.com.

'Through humor, you can soften some of the worst blows that life delivers'

Bill Cosby

13
A Fun theme tune

What should the theme tune be for all project managers?

Not one that was suggested in my survey below but I enjoyed the suggestion from the preceding PM Celebrity story:

I knew a project that had its own theme song – REM 'It's the end of the world (as we know it)'

Jon M Quigley

A while ago I ran a survey to find out the answer to this critical question and a large number of PMs out there in project management world climbed aboard the bandwagon and voted in their thousands.

At the end of stage one of the LinkedIn discussions I had 187 suggested tunes and by the end of the full campaign over 200 tunes. No one can argue that the project management musical taste was not a full and varied one for sure!

There was even a purpose built (or rather penned) offering in the shortlist from 'Mr IPM Day' himself, Frank Saladis - The Project Manager Blues (you can check that one out on YouTube). Beyond that we had suggestions ranging from classical to heavy metal and through punk and new wave and many more, such as 'Bob the Builder' and 'The Muppets' theme tunes.

So what were the results?

Number 1

The winner was, only just – it was a long battle between the top two songs throughout the competition – Mission Impossible by Lalo Schifrin.

It was congratulations to that old classic (I know there have been updates with Limp Bizkit and half of U2 but the original is still the best).

You know when this won out I thought 'hey that is a pretty negative song ... is that what all of my fellow PMs think? We are just trying to do something impossible?'

If you analyse the songs in the long list (and the shortlist) and broadly categorise them as:

• Positive/Optimistic
• Neutral/That is just life
• Negative/Depressive

Then you get a pretty even mix across the three categories. But if you do the same across the top ten songs then I would say that 80% were Positive/Optimistic.

Position	Song	% of overall vote
1	Mission Impossible – Lalo Schifrin/U2	6.16%
2	Under Pressure – Queen	6.11%
3	Always Look on the Bright Side of Life – Monty Python	4.93%
4	I will survive – Gloria Gaynor	3.59%
5	We are the Champions – Queen	3.08%
6	Communication Breakdown – Led Zeppelin	2.86%
7	My Way – Frank Sinatra/Sid Vicious	2.75%
8	Heroes – David Bowie	2.69%
9	Promised You a Miracle – Simple Minds	2.63%
10	Eye of the Tiger (theme from Rocky) – Survivor	2.52%

Maybe we should, on the basis of this book, add in a variation to the Cyndi Lauper classic 'PMs just wanna have fun'?

And then again, perhaps maybe not. Mission: Impossible was an American television series which chronicled the missions of a team of secret American government agents known as the Impossible Missions Force (IMF). The leader of the team was Jim Phelps, played by Peter Graves, except in the first season, during which the leader was Dan Briggs, played by Steven Hill.

A hallmark of the series shows Phelps receiving his instructions on a tape that then self-destructs, accompanied by the iconic theme music composed by Lalo Schifrin. I am pretty sure these days Health & Safety would not allow that but as a youngster it seemed a pretty exciting moment – instructions received and destroyed to protect the team.

The series aired on the CBS network from September 1966 to March 1973. It returned to television, as a revival, for two seasons on ABC, from 1988 to 1990 and later inspired a popular and commercially successful series of films starring Tom Cruise.

Project Impossible?

Whilst the title suggests an almost certain failure the IMF team never did fail (at least I can't remember them failing at all).

They planned meticulously and completed a risk assessment along with contingency actions before embarking on their extreme missions.

The plans always utilized the full range of skills in the team (the regular agent line-up during the first season consisted of Cinnamon Carter (Barbara Bain), a top fashion model and actress; Barnard 'Barney' Collier (Greg Morris), a mechanical and electronics genius and owner of Collier Electronics; William 'Willy' Armitage (Peter Lupus), a world record-holding weight lifter; Rollin Hand (Martin Landau), a noted actor, makeup artist, escape artist, magician and 'master of disguise' plus of course the leader of the team Mr Phelps, Jim Phelps (Peter Graves).

They used the latest and greatest equipment (OK so maybe they weren't working on a restricted budget) and throughout change management was a reality as the mission variables often depended on some smart out of the box thinking on the move.

And they delivered.

On time.

Each week!

So at the end of the day I salute all of you who voted for the Mission Impossible theme tune, a pretty damn good choice I would say.

It all started with me singing Monty Pythons' 'Always look on the bright side of life' and ended up with a new official and democratically selected tune to help each and every one of us in our day by day project activities.

This chapter will self-destruct in ten seconds time – Good Luck!

14
PM Celebrity Gossip – No win situations: Naomi Caietti

A long time ago in a galaxy far, far away there was a ship called the USS Enterprise ... we are talking about Project Management (PM) right?

As a kid growing up I loved watching science fiction shows like Star Trek. Why? They had a leader like James T. Kirk, a cool techie team and a space ship that would fly to far off distant planets. Kind of sounds like a project so far at least from my viewpoint working in Information Technology; always some infrastructure that needs repair or replacement.

Star Trek: The Movie introduced us to the no-win scenario in a training simulation called the Kobayashi Maru. Today's project manager's challenges require the performance of heroic feats to deliver projects that meet business needs, motivate team members and win over their stakeholders throughout the course of the project.

Let's take a trip to space to see how Captain Kirk would handle a project and see what lessons we can learn. Captain Kirk was a take charge kind of project manager let's ...he'd probably first meet with his top team members in his cabin; Spock, McCoy, Uhura, Sulu and Scotty prior to having a big meeting. He'd get a lot of logical ideas from Spock about what he was up against and he'd select him to act as a backup, McCoy would provide solutions and good medicine for some of problems he'd need to address, Uhura would provide insight into communication tactics, Sulu would provide recommendations on guidance and approach and Scotty, would have all the technical tools available when Kirk had finally motivated the team to take action to implement the iterations of the project and final solution.

Captain Kirk, would then take this information, hold his big meeting and go back and sit in his chair on the bridge surrounded by his leaders who were strong in the areas he was weak. The team would naturally be motivated by the flexibility of the leader to allow them to be creative and think of unconventional ways to approach the opportunity under considerable low odds to complete the mission.

Welcome to reality in many organizations, you have been given a project (mission), a PM role (ship to fly), a team (crew that doesn't report to you), no motivational benefits for the team (trips to other planets), lack of a sponsor (Starfleet) and an unseemingly no win assignment with (inadequate scope and high risk) low percentage outcome....cancelling the project is not an option.

This is truly a test of a leaders' character….. The better the leader understands their self, the better able they will be able to motivate and lead their teams in the face of conflict and uncertainty.

Well, also if you know how to program like Captain Kirk, this might help you to be a better leader and project manager.

Captain Kirk seemed to have it easy, pretty much in this case, he used a little ingenuity as well as if the team did not do their job the ship would crash in some far off distant planet.

A leader must consider what each person's motivation is to come to work every day. I don't know many people who come to work to sit at their desk every day but put them on a team and throw them in a room together and have them sit down with a PM; expect to run through a forming, storming, norming and performing cycle for a while.

My tips would be:

* Pick your superstars; they are self-motivated. Don't focus on the unmotivated at first; save your energy.
* Use your sphere of influence and let your leaders (superstars) lead
* Don't tolerate whiners, motivate them. Hint: These folks are usually your superstars, they want management's attention.
* Remove obstacles for your team; find ways to get them involved, and most of all give them recognition.
* Don't keep dead weight on your team.
* Empathize for a while and find out if they have anything to offer the team. If not, find someone else who can do the work.
* Be co-located with your team and listen to their concerns

Sometimes in the beginning it is not about the motivation, it's about the person and finding out what they can bring to the team. Many times it is the team who will motivate each other, not the project manager and finally if the project manager does not give up on the team it is the team who will not give up on the project manager and the project...it is time and synergy to let the team find its own motivations together.

Many times, I've found it is the project manager who has to show the team what Leadership is all about in the absence of other leaders in the organization...of course, I did not say it was easy...

'Character is the will to do what's right even when it's hard' Andy Stanley

Naomi Caietti engages with global project management communities on topics of leadership and Project Management as a published author, speaker, editorial board member, community manager, and blogger

through PMI Network, PMI Today, PMI Career Central, Employee Engagement, ProjectManagement.com, #PMChat, LinkedIn, Twitter (follow @califgirl232) and Projects@Work.com.

She is a credentialed project manager, consultant and enterprise architect who uses PMI, Agile, IEEE and other methodologies to assist customer and clients.

Naomi has also served on PMI-SVC Board of Directors and held other leadership roles for PMI Global Operations Center (GOC) at the local, regional and global level for a Component, Special, Member and Leadership Interest/Advisory Group. Listen, Empower, Adapt, Dream … LEAD!

'A smile is a facelift that's in everyone's price range'

Tom Wilson

15
A Fun team – Shell UK

Here we can gain some insight into the use of fun, humour, and a spirit of alternative ways of approaching some team building and skill acquiring activities that we have all faced in the past.

The following is a case study interview with Jeanette Yuile from Shell UK. The team, led by Jeanette, had certainly adopted a 'fun' approach to their project work and have seen some significant benefits from doing so.

[PT] Let's start with the introductions, Jeanette, tell us about yourself, the team, the projects and the objectives.

I work in Shell UK Limited as the Head of Sub-Surface and Wells Data Management for Europe and I lead large teams across Europe, mostly consisting of technical data managers. One of my teams is a dedicated project team of 15 people – known as the Log Data Improvement Project team (LDI). This is the most amazing team to work with and in addition to being excellent and very dedicated to what they do, they all have a great sense of humour that rivals any team I have worked with. Listing them by name they are; Andy Jones, Chris Reid, Jaisree Cavala, Rachel Shanks, John Lyth, Kieran Wall, Russell Crockett, Matthew Coleman, Simona Serban, Ewan Smart, Blair O'Connor, Bob Baxter, Jan Milne, Angus Dobbie and Julian Tice.

Our prime project objectives is to clean up very valuable legacy Log data and Pressure data and the team is in great demand by the business as they deliver such quality work in a smart way – lean processes and really powerful team work make it happen. I am very proud to lead them and the work they do account for huge savings in the millions for our 'Upstream' business.

[PT] I know that one of your first tasks was to sort of 'brand' the team members, to give then some identity. How did you approach this?

[JY] Smiley faces! All team members are allocated a smiley face by the PM (me) when joining the team – it creates an instant sense of belonging, puts a smile on everyone's face and makes for instant recognition of the team[28]. Our project sponsors have fully bought into the idea of 'fun at work' and all project team members display their smiley face with pride and joy in our project office area!

Everyone in a team also needs a common identity to bring them together and I chose rubber toys - Rubber flexible, hairy fronded and garishly coloured children's soft toys were just the answer. Pull them, stretch them, throw them – also good for stress relief. We take them out on Team meals, use them in Team photos – you know where you belong... and as a bonus, the project work gets done as well. Oh and your non project colleagues look on with bemused envy and curiosity, while your clients remember you for more than just your delivered excellent work products

[PT] Excellent, I may get you to select a suitable rubber toy for The Lazy Project Manager! What about team meetings, these can get pretty boring after a while, did you do anything here to make them more engaging for the team?

[JY] Absolutely. Team meetings occur once a week and can

---

28 Shell 'Fun' Team name check: Jeanette Yuile, Angus Dobbie, Andy Jones, Ewan Smart, Russell Crockett, Chris Reid, Kieran Wall, John Lyth, Bob Baxter, Jan Milne, Matthew Coleman, Simona Serban, Julian Tice, Jack Gooding, Alan Shanks. Alvaro Delgado Alvarado and Anjali Gondalia.

last anything from a brief half hour to a much lengthier hour and a half on special occasions. However, they are usually anything but dull…

At 11 o'clock on Thursday mornings, deputy PM Angus and Jeanette gather the team; we make ourselves tea and coffee and gather in 'the pod' where we settle into the soft circle of chairs.

Eyes are drawn to a cake box emerging from a plastic bag, or Tupperware pot filled with what looks like millionaire shortbread… Angus or Jeanette begins with an initial important catch up of any project developments, which is followed by contributions from team members on their progress throughout the last week. The meeting then takes a peculiar turn, fuelled by the presence of bakery items, interest in work related topics quickly fades and we descend into 'The Meltdown' and an exercise in social bonding begins.

Sure, a good forum on project matters is vital for our team to maintain the delivery of a top quality service that keeps the business machine well-oiled and running efficiently but for our team to function to the best of its potential; 'The Meltdown' is equally as important, if not more!

As we tuck into our cake it turns out its appearance at our meeting is a form of bribe from one team member to another, some sponge and cream encouragement to get a speedy send-off of some data to be read.

The weekly team meeting is the most frequent opportunity we get to delve into the lives of our colleagues outside of the workplace. As an example one team member, Blair, previously worked in mining in Australia where he saved hard and now has some money put aside that he would like to channel into an investment. His father owns some small holdings out past Inverness and, possibly inspired by his time in The Outback, Blair decided to buy some sheep for his father's farm. Forty-four sheep in total! He told us all about the costs and the possible return on his investment.

'I want to buy some sheep!' was my immediate reaction, but sadly the farm is already at full capacity and there is no more space for me to add to the flock. But I am on the look-out for other opportunities. PS: Blair has just left the team to finish his post grad degree in Geology, but he keeps in touch and joins us when he can for fun nights out etc.

[PT] Well I must say I have never had sheep crop up in any of my project meetings!

[JY] Discussions can take any direction each week and a variety of topics can be overheard by people passing by the pod; from home car maintenance to motorbikes, tractors, brewing beer and large screen 3D TVs, to fishing, horse riding, shoe fashion, Turkish masseuses, traditional dances of your native country and of course, the house training of pet rabbits. And we regularly catch up on the progress of Blair's sheep of course.

Longer meetings occur on birthdays where some gifts are exchanged, and we have an excuse for larger quantities of cake, including the opportunity to experience delights from other countries, such as Gajar Ka Halwa, a carrot based Indian sweet Jaisree made for Andy's 50th birthday. Much light hearted fun is had at the expense of the rapidly aging senior team member - '… but it's ok, because he won't remember by this time tomorrow!'- and so on but Mathew did get a very large homemade cake in the shape of a woman's corset, expertly decorated, and equally delicious!

[PT] Well I always say that coffee is on the critical path to project success but it seems cake should be there as well.

[JY] Always!

[PT] What about other team bonding activities, a team that plays well together works well together doesn't it?

[JY] I believe that is so true, one of the key contributors to fostering good project team spirit is socialising together and celebrating milestones, both professional and personal, as a group.

Usually we don't need an excuse to head out for a meal and some accompanying refreshments! These meals can take the form of more formal affairs with our project sponsors to celebrate project milestones etc. We give them a flavour of what we are about as a team, showcase our team ethos and get our sponsors buy-in to our project delivery methods and also use the engagements to secure future project opportunities for the team. At these dinners we have exposed our sponsors many hilarities; they have joined in the fun whole-heartedly and let their hair down - we have for example been getting our senior sponsors to wear paper plates on their ears, rabbit teeth and singing on top of their voices, all resulting in better bonding between team and sponsors and increasing trust.

Other times we organise full on crazy, informal team nights out where we celebrate birthdays, welcome new joiners to the team or toast and bid farewell to team members moving on to pastures new (although we know they will return the fold, they always do in the end!).

Another fun part of these evenings are the accompanying gifts bought by the team, sometimes serious but more often not so serious and they play a big part in the general hilarity. Gifts can range from a tasteful memento to remind someone moving away of the local area to full, ritual humiliation – woolly ski hat, oversize novelty sunglasses, cut off Tee-shirt and garish loud boxer shorts which all must be worn over normal cloths for the duration of the night out!

On a serious note (yes really) these nights out together, away from the work environment, really allow people working together as a project team to get to know the colleagues they work with on a daily basis (and some they don't!) and this only helps when returning to the office.

Projects Teams are made up of people who are of course all different but by knowing, understanding and acknowledging these differences it allows everyone to work together better towards our common goal.

[PT] I totally agree. Now a while ago I ran a survey to find out the perfect project management theme tune (you can find the results in this book) and I know that you also moved towards the musically direction at one team building event?

[JY] You are right. But why don't I let my deputy PM and our team musician Angus Dobbie tell you all about that

[AD] While at a team building event I've always thought the single most de-motivating and depressing thing to hear is 'we want to come up with a Team Song'- cue an awkward team activity of roughly bodging lines together through the butchered tune of some terrible pop song, with the activity culminating in the cringe worthy singing session where your 'song' is recited to the group. There really can be little worse. So when I was helping organise a team build event and heard the line 'I want to do some team songs' from Jeanette then I really didn't hold out much hope of anything good coming as a result.

Unfortunately for me Jeanette knew I was a bit of a musician so I was unduly assigned to come up with some songs that could be used to inspire the teams with writing their own. Now I said I was a 'bit of a musician' for a reason, it is true that I have played guitar and performed in a number of local bands but this was done in a spectrum of styles ranging from 'Heavy Rock' at the lighter end to full on 'Extreme Death Metal' at the other. Pop-based, radio friendly, corporate themed songs don't normally fall into this range. To add further insult to injury I was presented with a copy of several ABBA lyric sheets with the comment 'maybe you can do something with these'... oh joy!

The idea was I would perform my songs to the team with only my guitar as accompaniment. This was quite a daunting prospect, although I'd played some fairly difficult gigs in the past in rough pubs to rougher audiences, I'd always been with a band and had the advantage of not knowing the audience. Add to this the suggested choice of music I was somewhat out of my comfort zone, no-one to fall back on and an audience of my team mates who have to endure the worst activity we could throw at them. No pressure there then!

I spent some time thinking on what I could write, even enduring 30 seconds of an ABBA track to try and find some inspiration. The pop route was drawing blanks, writing a song from scratch wasn't working, this needed something more. One thing that kept returning to my thoughts was a scene from the film 'School of Rock' with Jack Black. In the film the main character, a fake school teacher, is put on the spot and pressured into playing a song he had written for a full band. With only his guitar the teacher plays out the whole stage act, setting the scene with imaginary dry ice and lighting and adding air drums and backing singers. Plus the song had the Holy Grail that every song writer of dreams about, an awesome sing-a-long chorus with suitably generic but not boring lyrics. This, I thought, had potential, ABBA was binned, the guitar was out and the rock was turned up! Steering away from the usual team song themes of promoting company values I decided to simply tell the story of how the team came into being with added rock exaggeration before bursting into the same awesome chorus as used in film. This was much more in my comfort zone and now I could perform the song with enough enthusiasm to inspire!

[PT] Hey fantastic project management is the new rock 'n' roll!

And Jeanette what do senior management make of all of this 'fun' stuff going on?

[JY] My own boss George Rorie, Europe/Africa Support & Deployment Manager, has this to say about the LDI team:

'The Log Data Improvement project team was originally people from different backgrounds, skills and experience. In theory they were working as a team, but sufficient attention had not been given to what motivated them - we were too busy looking at statistics, resolving quality issues, or arguing over contracts. We took some tough decisions, and made a fresh start, and gave them the opportunity to shape the way they worked, together with a new project manager - Jeanette. We took time to listen, and learn what individuals were passionate about and could bring to the team. The results were noticeable immediately and continued well beyond expectations. The first thing to change was the mood; people were smiling and excited about what they were doing. The improvement in delivery came a few weeks later and then kept improving. That was almost 3 years ago. Since then the team has grown, and only a few of the original team remain, but they continually on-board new members, develop individuals, watch them succeed and move on to new opportunities. However, the spirit has deepened, people are genuinely sorry to leave... most describe it as the best and most productive time in their careers so far.'

[JY] Our customers; Senior Managers in the business, just love the LDI team and here are quotes from a couple of them:

Kathy Heller; Chief Petrophysics, Upstream International Operated (she is also our business champion and business funding approver of our projects):

'It is a pleasure to work the LDI team. The LDI team Delivers, again and again, on time - on budget - good quality. And most importantly they make work fun. I'm convinced our performance everywhere could improve if we learned from this wonderful, high performing team!

Alan Johnson, Principal Petrophysicist, CNNS Asset:

'The LDI project was initiated to establish a fully QC'd data base, covering the majority of Shell acquired subsurface wireline log data going back to the 1970s. Over the years data had been stored in quite a piecemeal way and significant data gaps and inconsistencies had frequently been noted.

This data was acquired at considerable cost and, if lost, were effectively irreplaceable. The value delivered by this project was therefore potentially immense, but the process itself promised, at face value, to be intrinsically tedious and uninspiring. The challenge was therefore; how to maintain team motivation and focus throughout the years of these projects? The injection of unusual project management methods and maintaining a high level of fun interaction within in the team, and between the team and their customers, led not only to a highly motivated team but, equally important, to the successful delivery of a fully QC'd and complete data sets on, which the company can confidently use as the basis for its well and field interpretations going on well into the future'

[PT] Well all of the 'fun' seems to have paid off with real business and project results.

[JY] Absolutely, production has gone up by 30% since we started having some more fun – a great example that fun is not a time waster, but actually adding greatly to any project bottom line.

[PT] That is great to hear. And to finish off maybe one last story of something unusual that you instigated at Shell?

[JY] Oh that would have to be the 'Piggy Snatch' incident.

[PT] OK, that has got me intrigued, do go on.

[JY] Good team work starts from the project manager in any project and in this case it meant me supplying the team with a rubber pig mascot?

[PT] As you do.

[JY] And this story happened when I was away by the way.

[PT] So whilst the cat was away...

[JY] The mice did play, yes.

One Monday morning the team received a threatening email from 'thepiggysnatcher' the demanding email read 'More cake needed at next team meeting, or the pig gets it' and attached was a photo of our beloved team mascot pig trapped in the kidnapper's car. This had to be an insider job – but who could have done the dastardly deed?

The Team leapt in to action and used digital photo file properties to provide GPS co-ordinates that placed location of the kidnapper but then threats to 'back off' were made and a pig ear came through the post, followed by photo of a bandaged pig.

More daily emails followed with photos showing proof of life and the threat of a hot and smoky BBQ end for poor piggy if the cake demands were not met.

Negotiations failed and with the power of Smart-phones technology it meant no one could say who really the dastardly insider in the team was.

Finally the Friday team meeting came, with the usual offering of cake, but when the assembled masses returned to their desks, a final email from 'thepiggysnatcher' had arrived saying 'Damn, the pig made an escape'.

The pig mascot made his way back to the Project Team base and was found, neatly tucked up, un-harmed in his favourite place none the worse for his ordeal.

And when the cat got back, the story all had to be replayed in all of its hilarious glory, proving that mice too know how to play now.

[PT] A happy ending then, both for the fun team and for the pig; thank you for sharing some of the stories from your team. How about one piece of advice for other project managers and team members?

[JY] Happy people definitely deliver better quality work and having fun at work really makes a huge difference to both productivity and motivation. It's all about getting the job done, but having fun doing it!

I like these two quotes as it sums up the importance of team work;

'Coming together is a beginning. Keeping together is progress. Working together is success'

and

'The nice thing about teamwork is that you always have others on your side!'

16
PM Celebrity Gossip – Team building with consequences: Gary 'Gazza' Nelson

On my first major project, I was assigned to work with the onsite project team in Hamilton, New Zealand for a couple years as an on-site technical resource. It was my first overseas trip, and first time working in another country. It was a great learning experience, and as you might expect, we all had a bit of initial culture shock. Many things were very similar to Canada, as New Zealand is an English-speaking Commonwealth country.

However, one of the differences we had some difficulty with was in pronouncing the local Maori place names. (To be fair, our New Zealand clients also had similar difficulties in pronouncing indigenous place names in Canada.) To help all new project members when they came on-site, they received a brief lesson in pronouncing Maori names.

Some history: Maori was originally only a spoken language, but an early European settler worked with them and formed a written alphabet so the language could be recorded. He based it on the English alphabet, with a few differences – rather than muck about with the dual-sound letter 'C', which can sound like 'S' or 'K', he got rid of it. He also left out the letter 'F' – replacing it with 'WH' to be sounded out as 'F'. The pronunciation of several vowels was also different than English – 'e' is often more like the long 'a' – for example, 'Te

Awamutu' is pronounced 'Tay Ah-wah-moo-too'.

We usually used Ngaruawahia as the final pronunciation and spelling test – it was a town we drove through between the airport and the customer site, and a very difficult word.

So – everyone received their mini language lesson on arrival, and we all tried our best and gradually were able to pronounce most of the names fairly reasonably.

About two and a half years on into the project (a year and a half after I arrived), the major deliverables had been deployed, and the initial Project Manager and his assistant moved back to Canada when their contacts ended. A replacement Project Manager was brought in for the next year to support the installation. While the first Project Manager was a bit crusty around the edges with lots of battle scars, the replacement PM was quite bright, eager and full of enthusiasm. It was not youth – he was nearly as close to retirement as the prior PM. It was just his personality – he was very easy going and always inquisitive.

In the first week, we gave him his Maori language pronunciation lesson. He paid very close attention, and practiced it at every opportunity – he wanted to make a good first impression with the customer.

However, he was a bit over-zealous.

On Thursday of his first week, we went out for lunch and walked through the local mall. We went into a local bookstore (Whitcoulls), where he selected a book for purchase. When he went up to pay for the book, he asked the clerk if the store was pronounced 'Fitcools'.

The clerk looked at him strangely and said 'No, it is pronounced Whit-cools, it is an English name.'

This gave us an idea to play a trick on our new (hopefully forgiving, easy-going) PM. Did I say forgiving?

When someone new arrived, we usually went on a road-trip their first weekend, to show them the sights. So we arranged for the four of us that were still on-site, including the PM, to go spend Saturday in Auckland, which was about an hour and a half away. We left early, to make the most of the day.

On the drive up, as we passed some of the most beautiful, lush scenery you will ever see, we told our new PM that we had this fantastic restaurant that we planned to take him to, pronounced 'Tah-kay-ah-way' – but it would depend on the timing of the day's activities. If we ran late, we would have to skip it.

About half way there the PM called out the name of a road sign he saw, practicing his Maori as much as he could. 'Rack-eh-koor-say' he said proudly. I looked at the sign. I shook my head. 'Racecourse – that's another English sign,' I said. He lost the smile.

We had fantastic clear early autumn weather – it was a perfect day. The rest of us had a substantial lunch but the PM only ordered a small meal. We saw quite a few sights during the day, Kelly Tarleton's Underwater World, downtown Auckland, One Tree Hill and North Head. It was a lot of walking, and by the end of the afternoon we were all getting fairly hungry. The PM was getting impatient though – he was quite hungry from only having the small lunch, and he said was really looking forward to this fancy restaurant we kept talking about.

It reached a point where we were still trying to enjoy the view after walking all the way up the hill at North Head, when the PM was urging us onward. He wanted to make sure we had time for dinner at this fancy place! So of course, we took our time getting back to the car. Our easy-going PM was getting a bit frazzled. 'Hurry up, hurry up!'

We all piled into the car and drove over to the other side of Auckland, close to the motorway on the way back to Hamilton. We pulled up in front of a small shop, parked the car and turned off the ignition.

'Where is it? Where is it?' asked the PM.

I pointed straight ahead. 'Right there.'

As he turned his head and followed my pointed finger he read the sign while the others in the car just smiled:

'TAKEAWAY'

Fish & Chips

It was the first time we heard our PM swear! 'You bastards! You had me going all day long! My stomach was preparing for a gourmet 5-course meal. This is just Fish and Chips!'

'You can get Chinese food too,' I suggested. He just glared at me.

Fortunately, our PM did have a sense of humour – it came back after about three weeks. In the meantime he put us through hell with all sorts of menial tasks. But it was worth it!

Lesson: Team-building exercises come in many forms, if you can handle the consequences!

Gary M Nelson, PMP (Gazza) is the author of Gazza's Guide to Practical Project Management and the upcoming children's PM book, The Ultimate Tree House Project, which teaches basic Project Management concepts to school age children ages 7-10. Gary is an IT consultant and Project Manager who has worked in the Telecom and Student Information Systems sectors since 1989. His international experience includes projects in New Zealand, Taiwan, Hong Kong, the US and Canada. Gary enjoys speaking and training, and employs experience-based stories to communicate complex concepts to audiences of all skill levels. This approach is reflected in both his in-person training style and his writing, which includes Gazza's Corner Project Management Blog and Podcast.

17
A Fun team – IHG

The following is from Crystal Snoddy who heads up Delivery Excellence for the global IHG® Programme Office. Crystal and the Programme Office team have definitely been applying some innovative approaches to project management development.

[PT] Crystal firstly why don't you tell us all about your role, your team and IHG?

[CS] Of course Peter, I head up the Delivery Excellence Team at IHG - InterContinental Hotels Group.

IHG is one of the world's largest global hotel companies, with well-known global brands such as InterContinental® Hotels and Resorts, Crowne Plaza® Hotels and Resorts, and Holiday Inn®. We have over 4,600 hotels spanning almost 100 countries and employ over 345,000 people across our owned, managed and franchised estate.

It is a growing business that celebrates its 10th year as a standalone company. Our BrandHearted culture is grounded in hospitality and has an entrepreneurial atmosphere, which are central to both driving a great guest experience and attracting new hotel owners. For us, hospitality is about being genuine and caring; it is about each of us welcoming and exceeding our guests' expectation every time. We want not only our guests' loyalty to our brands but also their love. In fact, that is our measurement of success; we measure 'Great Hotels Guests Love'.

Our company's vision is to become one of the world's greatest companies. In order to reach this vision, we need to have a culture that delivers change swiftly. Our Global Programme Office works closely with the regional and functional Programme Offices to help align the organisation behind our brands, and allow for efficiencies and focus on our highest priority initiatives through our integrated delivery plan.

IHG views projects as a vehicle to foster a change culture and as such we put a great deal of care into both the projects we select and the methods we use to deliver them.

[PT] Excellent so what is different about the way that IHG approach projects to most other organisations do you think?

[CS] We start by looking at change as a cultural mind-set. We approach our 'IHG Way' of Delivery by looking at three aspects:

The project manager community – this includes their skills, attitudes and ability to connect and learn from themselves and one another.

The project management methodology and tools – which includes equipping our project managers and leaders with appropriate tools, templates and change methods that tangibly support a tailored approach to delivering change at IHG

IHG Delivery Standards which establish minimum standards to be delivered and enforced regardless of tools used or project type

Another aspect that makes IHG's delivery approach unique is that we put great attention on incorporating balanced thinking into everything we do.

[PT] Balanced thinking?

[CS] Yes. The basis of balanced, or 'whole-brained' thinking suggests that we all have preferred ways of thinking and behaving influenced by different parts of our brain (logical and linear vs. creative and innovative for example). Though there is value to all thinking styles we are not all holistic thinkers by nature. In fact, only 2% of the world's population uses the quadrants of the brain equally. The remaining 98% of us have thinking 'preferences' that influence the way we think and approach to how we solve problems. These preferences often become more obvious or may alter slightly under stress. Project management by its very nature of deadlines and introducing 'new' ways of working puts individuals under stress. Understanding this equips our project managers to skillfully navigate the waters of change; which means to help individuals, to align team members and to ultimately introduce authentic change that sticks.

[PT] I see. Can you give some examples of this approach?

[CS] Sure, let's start with our partnership of conventional project management with new approaches such as 'Pub Speak' & visual thinking.

Whether we are developing content for a guide, template or a project-related workshop, we use a language that is friendly, familiar and warm words to convey our message. We refer to this as 'Pub Speak'. Though we still use some of the 'tried and true' tools, we always refer to them simply and clearly, avoiding acronyms or anything that will introduce complexity. This seems simple but corporate culture tends to over complicate and this keeps a pulse on this behaviour.

In addition, we leverage the use of visual thinking. Our practice includes the use of pictures, animations, drawings and symbols whenever possible to communicate a simple visual message. For us, using visual thinking spans the globe and cuts across cultures. We also provide project managers visual thinking facilitation tools that are aimed at helping non-artists use visuals to break through complex problems in a group setting.

Our visual thinking tools have helped save IHG frustration, time and money. It is so much easier and effective to think, converse and explain complex concepts with pictures. To visualize is to understand; understanding drives alignment and alignment leads to faster group decision-making.

Today's business environment is changing, and fast. Today's project managers are faced with solving problems with new complexity, sophistication and interconnectedness. Traditional project management approaches that focus solely on standard linear thinking, update meetings and status reports are out dated and do not deal with the need to drive global collaboration and alignment.

There are many reasons that we use visual thinking but among some of these are:

Visual tool make understanding and solving complex problems easier. Drawing problems and solutions requires simplification and allows everyone to rally around one visual 'story'.

Visualizing a problem can surface emotional barriers to change that may not be addressed otherwise. Emotional barriers can be some of the most difficult to understand and yet the most paramount for making changes 'stick'.

Visual thinking helps people of varying cultures find a common language to align around. With hotels in over 100 countries, IHG is the embodiment of a global company. Finding ways to bring people together is paramount to our success.

Visual thinking also breaks through linear problem solving and creates a safe environment for out-of-the-box and innovative thinking

[PT] That all makes great sense to me, I am all for keeping it simple and effective. And how do you go about training your project managers in IHG?

[CS] Similar to other training programmes, our three-day expert training includes a facilitator lead presentation, group activities, and self-study homework. Unlike other training programmes, however, we also incorporate activities that target one's awareness of self and team; including personal assessments and participation 'improv' & cookery. Increasing our project manager's self-awareness is important to us. Even experts who already have the hard skills and experience needed to manage projects struggle with the soft skills needed to navigate the organisation. Increased self-awareness strengthens teamwork, which is critical to our success in this highly matrix organisation.

Prior to the training, each participant completes an online instrument on individual thinking preferences. During the training, we introduce the assessment and explain the results so that each member can understand not only their own unique thinking profile but also that of the other participants. We stress that there is no 'right profile, rather wonderful diversity that when accepted with a 'win- win' mind-set unlocks delivery.

For this, we incorporate a variety of group activities targeted at demonstrating the collective behaviour of varying group profiles. Though understanding one's own preference is a key first step, we take it further still to understanding pair profiles and team's group dynamics in order to increase chances of project success. Understanding self, pairs and group not only helps project managers build more effective balanced-thinking teams, but to foresee and mitigate stakeholders risks before they occur. As a result, acknowledging and incorporating style diversity has become part of the way we work.

Participating in improv workshops is also a part of our training that makes it unique. Performing improv is about building trust, increasing self- awareness and supporting 'in the moment' behaviours. Performers agree to the same set of rules and structure for each scenario. Every scenario is without script leaving participants to rely on each other in order to build and collectively create the scene. Good scenes are created when performers can let go of "control" and instead leverage each other to build something wonderful, and quite often very funny! This has proven a fantastic activity because you see spontaneity, creativity and trust emerge right before your eyes; three elements critical to the success of the project manager.

[PT] IT all sounds a lot of fun but how does improv and self-awareness help a project manager and their team?

[CS] It presents a different mind-set when interacting with people. The 'in the moment', accepting and harmonizing mind-set sharpens one's agility to act intuitively on any information or situation. Project management is real life, it is dynamic and people oriented; the more self-aware each member is, the more likely the project team will achieve success.

During one of the improv scenes, we introduce the concept and our culture of 'yes and...' The participants trial using 'yes and...' versus 'no, but' or 'yes, but....'

An improv comedian uses 'yes and' to build on their partners story. The moment 'yes but' or 'no but' enters the stage, the skit and the once opportunity for creativity dies. Visibly the group sees and feels how using 'yes, and....' creates a supportive, accepting, cultivating interaction. Using the language of 'Yes and...' instead of 'Yes, but...' or 'No but...' can turn any adversarial situation or interaction into a productive one. 'Yes and...' is part of our collaborative culture.

And we have had some great feedback from this. One comment received recently... 'The Improv session was great, a real 'Ah-ha' moment... it's really made me open my eyes to how I can work with people in a different, much more collaborative way'.

[PT] That is great feedback and I love the alternative approach, I often feel like a stand-up comic at some of my presentations and now I know I need to try out improv as well.

You mentioned cooking was part of the expert training as well?

[CS] On one of the evenings, the group ventures out to a cookery school for a unique team building activity, this illustrates the essence of teams and the practice of project management. With a brief orientation to the kitchen, the cookery's executive chef 'project sponsor' gives high-level requirements, time limits and general guidance with expectations for each of the dishes' deliverables' on the menu 'project'. The group is divided into cooking teams 'project teams' and each instructed to work independently.

There is a little light-hearted competition and the fruit of everyone's labour is experiencing the dishes together as our evening meal. We start the next morning discussing what the participants experienced during the cookery and how it relates to every day challenges of project management. Using cookery as a metaphor for project environments has proven very effective in providing a neutral foundation for discussing some of project managers' most delicate topics.

[PT] Brilliant, and as you say everyone gets there rewards in form of a meal at the end, as well as a pretty special learning experience. Do you have any definitive benefits from all of this great work? Executives always like a few points of proof from such investment don't they?

[CS] We have quite a few success stories.

One example that comes to mind is a project that selected, configured and deployed a quality inspection automation system and optimized the inspection process globally. Some of the results of that project include:

- It successfully aligned key quality elements and enabled the company to look at quality across all of our brands and the regions with like-to-like data for the first time.
- This project reduced annual web application hosting costs by 60%

- Through automation, we reduced auditing time by 2 hours per audit for our General Managers and consultants (25. With 6000 quality evaluations per year this equals over 24,000 hours saved

Other examples include:
- Hotel Solutions (an internally developed expert system that assists general managers and hotel staff identify tools to help them solve hotel issues and serves as a forum to share ideas.
- IHG Green Engage® (an internally developed and hosted system that helps hotels identify and deploy cost effective solutions to make their hotels more environmentally friendly while lower operating costs):
  o Holiday Inn® Waikiki Beachcomber Resort reduced energy consumption by 4,000 kWh per day and saved 624,267 gallons of water annually through improved cooling tower operations.
  o InterContinental® Barclay New York Hotel- The hotel began recycling and composting; saving an average of $1,500 per month due to recycling, and $600 per month due to composting. Switching to all incandescent light bulbs saved $138,600 annually within a payback period of 4 months and had a return on investment of approximately 238%.
  o Holiday Inn Express® - Airport Hotel replaced 2 gas fired boilers in 2010 & have had a consistent 25% natural gas reduction year over year, which has helped reduce total energy by 11% year over year.

In addition to these results, we are seeing results that our employees are enjoying the IHG Way of Project Delivery and feeling engaged in delivering change to IHG, making IHG a great place to work:

'I was blown away the attention to detail put into this initiative. This will be a mandatory development for my teams and will become a way of interaction for us. Kudos to you and the PMO!'

'The session helped me understand myself, and understand how to best work with others'

'The toolkit is great - it means that you have something tangible to help you through the phases - and I think it will encourage people more to actually used the visual tools and the templates'

'It is good to hear a consistent central message that teams can go off and apply. Excellent supporting material/collateral also to stop people reinventing the wheel'

[PT] Many thanks for sharing this Crystal and I wish you all the best for the future. Do you have perhaps one last tip for other project managers or PMO leaders out there?

[CS] Introducing change in today's world requires more than conventional project management. Change is about winning the hearts and minds of people and their genuine commitment to move in a common direction. The 'IHG Way' to Project Delivery has been a team effort and has required a multi-year commitment and passion from our team and from IHG's executive leadership.

I would recommend looking at conventional project management with a new creative and whole-brained lens. Consider new approaches that incorporate visual thinking, behaviour/thinking style tools and ways of building a 'yes and' attitude - this will go a long way to introducing 'winning change'.

Crystal Snoddy heads up the Delivery Excellence Team. For over 20 years, she has led people, processes, and projects in way that improves productivity and promotes innovation and growth.

Crystal credits her passion for art, human behavioural sciences and change management for her unique mind-set when facing business challenges. Understanding that competitive advantage often relies on a team's ability to connect, share, and effectively respond to ideas, Crystal and her team have been the driving force behind creation of the 'IHG Way' of Project Delivery; new and unique approach to producing business results.

Outside work, Crystal's passions combine skiing, Latin dance, volunteering with the non-English and refugee population, and travelling to unknown places. You will find that elements of her passion in the form of creativity, adventure, collaboration and making a difference have all found their way into IHG projects. And while attendees of the new IHG Way training don't get out on the ski slope or on the dance floor, they might experience a touch of cookery and theatre, as well as other engaging and fun ways to approach their work.

18
PM Celebrity Gossip – Avoiding check-box fun: Robert Kelly

As a consultant, I have had the opportunity to work across a lot of companies and multiple groups within those firms. In my nomadic career, I have worked with dozens of managers and watched their decision making, strategy planning, personnel development and team building skills. Unfortunately, there isn't much creativity when it comes to team building and injecting fun into the organization or project team. Going out to lunch, taking the team bowling or some form of food gathering (pizza, ice cream social, etc) seems to be the standard options and unfortunately, the feedback is that it often feels like a check-box the manager is trying to check off. In addition to what I feel was a successful event, I have been impressed with the folks at AtTask and the dodge ball challenge they implemented in 2012.

In an attempt to think outside the box and within a limited budget, I took a team to a local family fun centre where we could enjoy some food and drinks, followed by laser tag, bumper cars, rock climbing, batting cages and more. The group had been working together for a while, but didn't connect with one another and weren't really collaborating. The thought was that some light food and drinks would loosen folks up and the games would bring out the competitive child in each of us. Plus, who doesn't want to shoot the boss... albeit with a laser tag gun.

This sort of environment really got people to leave the office behind and let loose. The real key to the success was not just attending and taking care of the bill, but being a host to introduce people and planning out the teams to ensure people from different functions were working together and building those bonds. This sort of event also provided some long lasting laughs and discussions in the office, whether it was something they discussed over drinks, how they all 'got the boss', or talked a little office trash for the next time they went go-carting.

And make sure you have a designated photographer. It certainly helped to have assigned someone to take some pictures of the team throughout the day, which served as some fun to recap during meetings and include in newsletters.

Robert Kelly is the Founder and Managing Partner of Kelly Project Solutions in Raleigh, NC, USA. Robert has managed a wide-range of projects initiatives at some of the world's leading organizations, including Morgan Stanley, Credit-Suisse, Lenovo, and Red Hat. His diverse experience includes new product development, IT Services, software development, global vendor selection, and demand waterfalls with benefits realization in over 40 countries. Robert is also the co-founder of #PMChat, a global community of project managers that collaborate on leadership and project management best practices, via numerous social media platforms. In addition to being a speaker and blogger, Robert has been featured on FastCompany's 30 Second MBA and in PMI's PMNetwork Magazine.

19
A Fun final word

So there you have it, unequivocal proof that project managers do have a sense of humour and that project management can be fun. I can't really say it any better than this.

I surely know that even in the most serious situation smiling delivers the best outcome as the team understands that the project manager has confidence in them and that a positive way out of any such situation can be found. Smiling is healthy and can help a project manager think clearer and keep the team closer to him or her, and usually a joke to get people to smile is all it needs. In the end we are there to make the impossible possible!

Anca Popa

Oh yes Anca, I think (like Miss Anne Elk[29]) you have hit the nail on the head there. As I only said myself a hundred or so pages earlier 'It's kind of not possible to not do the fun when you're trying to do the impossible, or something close to the impossible'.

This book has hopefully provided you with some new ideas and new (and perhaps not so new) jokes. It has aimed to offer up some inspirational thoughts from other project managers through quotes, suggestions and anecdotes. You have heard

---

29 I am referring to Miss Anne Elk's Theory on Brontosauruses which is a sketch from Monty Python's Flying Circus in an episode that features Graham Chapman as a television interviewer and John Cleese in drag as a palaeontologist, Anne Elk, appearing in a television talk show titled Thrust. The Lazy Project Manager book leans heavily on what I refer to as the 'dinosaur' theory of projects.

from myself as well as a number of project management superstars that are far better at this project management thing than I ever will be. And you have been invited in to look at two different but equally uplifting and idea generating case studies from two project communities in major organisations.

It seems only right (and perhaps almost inevitable) that we finally end up with that classic 'fun' proclamation about project management that appears in so many places that perhaps we will never know who first put this thought together – enjoy and not only 'be lazy' but have a bloody good laugh whilst you are doing it.

The Plan

In the beginning there was the plan and the plan was good.

But then came the assumptions, and the assumptions were without form and the plan was completely without substance and the darkness was upon the faces of the employees.

And they spake amongst themselves, saying 'It is a crock of shit and it stinks!'

And so the employees went unto their supervisors, saying 'It is a pail of dung and none may abide the odour thereof.'

Thereafter the supervisors went unto their division managers, saying 'It is a vessel of fertilizer and none may abide its strength.'

And the division managers went unto their general manager, saying 'It contains that which aids plant growth and it is very strong.'

And soon the general manager went unto the Board, saying 'It promotes growth and is very powerful', adding 'This new plan will actively promote the growth and efficiency of this organization.'

And so it came to pass that the Board looked upon the plan and saw that it was good and so the Plan became Policy.

This is how s**t happens!

You know you often see
'This page has been left
blank for a reason' and
you wonder why? Well this
page has been left blank
and there is a very good
reason ...

Appendix 1
The Giant Killer-Carrot of Death

Well you have been patient and so this is the story that I keep referring to, and that you can find referred to in my book *The Lazy Project Manager* (Infinite Ideas).

There was a time when I cared what others thought about me but that time has mostly passed; I still care a little of course.[30]

I think a significant turning point came a few years ago, not too many years ago come to think of it, when I was working on a global program within my own company. The program was simple in its concept – develop a standard project management methodology, train everybody in that methodology, and then make sure that everyone used the methodology all of the time.

Parts one and two (develop and train) were not without their challenges but were achieved within 12 months, which was pretty good going. Part three proved to be the really difficult part. We met with not resistance as such but more apathy and a general mood of 'just smile politely and they will eventually leave us alone to carry on as we have always done'. Adoption rates were low and we were failing.

We had many (many) discussions, workshops, conference calls, brainstorming sessions and the like to try and work out what could be done to drive adoption that much faster. And all these ideas pretty much fell in to two camps – the incentive category (or carrot) and the punishment category (stick).

---

30 Editor's note: Oh he still cares. Just check out how upset he gets when he gets a bad review for one of his books (so be gentle with him on this one).

One aspect of working on a global project was that conference calls, amongst the team, were often held at unusually early or late calls, and on one of these late long calls I finally had had enough.

As the conversation went around and around the carrot and stick, stick and carrot, all carrot and no stick, all stick and no carrot options I suddenly stated ' What we actually need is the Giant Killer Carrot of Death'.

Silence.

Laughter.

'Oh we'd pay to see that' came the general response and so, two weeks later, and having secured a suitable costume I was outside my house having my photograph taken in a giant bright orange and green carrot costume (I was very surprised when I contacted a large fancy dress costume hirers and requested a vegetable outfit. They listed a quite impressive list of options of both the vegetable and fruit variety).

And so it came to pass that the 'Giant Killer Carrot of Death' began his (do carrots have a gender?) reign of driving adoption in the methodology.

I really don't think that the whole root vegetable thing helped in any way with the future adoption levels but it certainly made the team laugh and gave them all a great introduction to many conversations, meetings and presentations after that (with the highest 'laugh' factor being the ones where they did this when I was also in the room):

'Have you seen Peter dressed as a carrot?'

I like to think I made a few people's working day a little lighter.

So there you have it, the whole 'root vegetable' thing and yes there is a picture of this.

What?

You want to see it?

Well I guess since I am proposing that fun is important and there is no disgrace in making a fool of yourself for the greater good of the project team I can't refuse can I?

No.

So here goes.

Ready?

Sure?

There is no going back on this once you have seen it.

Last chance.

OK.

Now ... Just turn the page!

And just to put my carrot costume in to some context, do you remember the 'blondies' in Fun Motivation? Well here they are in all of their glory (beautiful...) – enjoy:

Appendix 2
Peter Taylor

Peter in his more normal setting of sitting in the comfy chair rather than pretending to be a root vegetable

Peter Taylor is the author of two best-selling books on 'Productive Laziness' – *The Lazy Winner* and *The Lazy Project Manager.*

In the last 3 years he has focused on writing and lecturing with over 200 presentations around the world in over 20 countries and with new books out including *The Lazy Project Manager and the Project from Hell, Strategies for Project Sponsorship, Leading Successful PMOs*, and *The Thirty-Six Stratagems: A Modern*

Interpretation of a Strategy Classic – with a number of other book projects currently underway.

He has been described as 'perhaps the most entertaining and inspiring speaker in the project management world today' and he also acts as an independent consultant working with some of the major organizations in the world coaching executive sponsors, PMO leaders and project managers.

His mission is to teach as many people as possible that it is achievable to 'work smarter and not harder' and to still gain success in the battle of the work/life balance.

More information can be found at:
www.thelazyprojectmanager.com, www.thelazywinner.com and www.leadingsuccessfulpmos.com – and through his free podcasts in iTunes.

Why not book Peter for your organisation:
* Keynote Presentations and Lectures
* Master of Ceremonies
* Inspirational Workshops
* Coaching
* Customised Authoring

Appendix 3
The Lazy Project Manager

The following is an extract from *The Lazy Project Manager* (Infinite Ideas).

'I love deadlines. I love the whooshing noise they make as they go by'

Douglas Adams
(Author of *The Hitchhikers Guide to the Galaxy*)

You have to laugh; well I think you have to laugh.

Without a little bit of fun in every project then the project world can be a dark and depressing place.

Setting a professional but fun structure for your project can really be beneficial for when the problems start to rise up to challenge your plan of perfectness. And problems will inevitably arise.

In the years I have done many things to encourage team bonding, lighten the darker moments of project hell, and diffuse difficult project related situations. I have even accepted the full and complete blame for every problem, issue and challenge to a project in front of a room full of project team members, before walking outside and firing myself (in a loud voice, well voices – one mine and one me pretending to be my boss). The net result was a diffused situation, where it had previously been extremely confrontational between teams and individuals.

Done well this does not damage your status or authority but can actually be a very positive act in people seeing you a human being, and not just a project manager, and thereafter wanting to share a smile and a laugh with you during the day.

It is just the same in that hotbed of confrontation, the home!

Try looking at one of your children when they are in a really bad mood. Look them in the eye, with a serious face, and point a finger at them and say 'Don't laugh! Don't you dare laugh! If you laugh you will go straight to the naughty stair!' I bet at the very least you will get a smile out of them.

My family finds that, even in the most stressed out, aggressive, emotional and 'in your face' moments, if you can make the opposition (and I use that term loosely) laugh then the war is soon over.

It is hard to kill someone when you are laughing.

Well I guess that is true except for some of the more extreme psychopathic types ('No, I expect you to die Mr Bond' ... cue maniacal laughter).

Make fun part of your project:

We all know about the team phases, 'forming – storming – norming – performing – mourning'[31] – if you don't there is

---

31 The Forming – Storming – Norming – Performing model of group development was first proposed by Bruce Tuckman in 1965, who maintained that these phases are all necessary and inevitable in order for the team to grow, to face up to challenges, to tackle problems, to find solutions, to plan work, and to deliver results. This model has become the basis for subsequent models of group development and team dynamics and a management theory frequently used to describe the behavior of existing teams. Tuckman later added a fifth phase, adjourning, that involves completing the task and breaking up the team. Others call it the phase for mourning.

plenty of information on the topic out there in 'Google-land'.

Now I would suggest that to have a little bit of fun can really help calm the nerves during the storming phase when team conflict and competition can be high; it should be indoctrinated in to the norming phase as the team develops their working rules and processes; and finally, during the performing phase I am convinced of the value of fun in keeping the team at peak performance.

Here are a few ideas:

Working with a Canadian colleague we used to put 'secret' fun messages in presentations that we each gave. This allowed us to have a laugh or two, and in fact challenged us to put more and more difficult words and phrases in to business presentations without anyone else spotting something odd was going on. I extended this to a full project team once. No one knew that the others were in the 'game'; everybody thought it was just them and me. It was very amusing. The meeting had a great feeling about it, everyone was happy and smiling. And yes, it was very productive.

You can do things like 'It's Friday' the one day of the week when the team care share 'funnies' through email.[32] This is good because it limits to a degree such emails to one day of the week and it should also make the team consider what is appropriate for general sharing rather than just sharing everything.

My current team all enjoy many happy moments, once a year, when we 'talk like a pirate' on, honestly, 'Talk like a Pirate' day'.[33] Check it out.

---

32 Check any policies that your company may have regarding non-business emails

33 This is not a joke, it is a real 'International Day' – www.talklikeapirate.com – have fun 'talking' like a pirate, using email 'translators' to create pirate speech communication, and even slap on an eye patch and a parrot to get in to the mood. Just for the one day you understand, any more than that and you are probably just odd.

Practice safe fun:

Obviously it has to be acceptable fun – don't want to be 'pc' here but do be careful – think carefully about your team members, does your fun equal other people's fun?

Also bear in mind there are times to have fun and times to be serious, you and your team must understand the parameters of this. And there may be members of the project team who just don't want to have fun, make sure that they are not excluded or isolated from the rest of the team.

Make your fun smart fun:

Now, when you have this whole 'work hard but have some fun' project underway the smart, and by that I of course mean 'productively lazy' project managers, will sit back in the comfy chair and let their project team self-generate the fun working atmosphere.

Done right you will have set the acceptable parameters for fun in your project, both in content and in extent, and you will have engendered that spirit amongst your project team to the point where, one day, when you are the one on a low, they will make come up and make you smile.

Have fun on your projects. '

And no Mr Bond, I expect you to laugh'

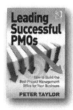    

THE FUNNY ENDING

62111792R00086

Made in the USA
Lexington, KY
29 March 2017